MARY FORD

CAKE RECIPES

MARY FORD

D0276112

INTRODUCTION

All of my books in the 'Classic step-by-step series" have focussed on the decoration and presentation of cakes and the various techniques associated with this aspect of the craft. Over the years, I have come across so many delicious recipes I felt it appropriate to put my favourites together in a book so they could be made and enjoyed by a wider audience.

Making and baking cakes is one of the most rewarding aspects of cookery, and the results are (almost!) always greatly admired and appreciated. In choosing the cakes for the book I have selected those with readily available ingredients for occasions when preparation and cooking time is limited. I hope that it becomes apparent when using the book that making delicious cakes can be fast and fun, and is more a question of assembling the correct ingredients and following the instructions than of being an experienced cake maker. I make no apologies for starting the book with the "old favourites" of sponge, genoese and a basic fruit cake. These are all such versatile recipes for the base of any cake that no cake recipe book would be complete without them. The remaining cakes will, I hope, appeal to the most diverse tastes ranging from ginger cake to sachertorte. I have included for some of them a "Mary's tips" section to highlight a particular variation, technique or idea I have used.

I hope you enjoy these cakes as much as I have.

ACKNOWLEDGEMENTS

My thanks are due to Royal Worcester Limited and Rachel John for the loan of numerous plates and other items of china. Throughout the text the Royal Worcester name for the design used in the photograph appears in the style "**CHANTILLY GOLD**". The plate design used on the cover photograph is "**SUMMERFIELD**".

I would also like to thank Prestige Group UK PLC for the cake tins and other cooking utensils used in the preparation of the cakes.

© Copyright Mary Ford Publications Ltd and Mary Ford Books Ltd.

Published 1993 by Mary Ford Publications Ltd.

Typesetting: Avant Mode Ltd – Bournemouth
Manufactured by Supreme Publishing Services.
Printed and bound by star standard, Singapore.
ISBN: 0 946429 43 X

AUTHOR

Mary Ford has been teaching the art of cake-making and decorating for three decades. Working with her husband, Michael, she has produced over twenty step-by-step books demonstrating the various skills and techniques of the craft. Her books have gained a worldwide reputation for expertise and imagination combined with common sense and practical teaching ability. Her unique step-by-step approach with the emphasis on self-explanatory colour illustrations is ideally suited for both beginners and enthusiasts.

CONTENTS

GETTING STARTED

THE RECIPES

Begin by reading the recipe through from beginning to end, checking you have all the listed ingredients in the correct quantities, and all the necessary cooking equipment. Make sure you have enough time to complete the preparation and cooking. If you intend to adjust the quantities of the recipes, for instance to make more than one cake, then take special care with your calculations. Although doubling the ingredients for twice the quantity may work for some cakes, it may be disastrous with others. Unfortunately there is no hard and fast rule for this, and the only answer is to try a dummy run before you make a large cake for a special occasion. If in doubt, I would strongly recommend you stick to the quantities given, as these have produced proven cakes.

INGREDIENTS

In certain recipes it can happen that cold ingredients can curdle the cake mixture. Consequently, about an hour before starting to cook, or more for a fruit cake, assemble all the ingredients and leave them to stand at room temperature. This is particularly important for butter and margarine, which will be far easier to work with when it is slightly soft.

Most shops and all supermarkets now have a very wide choice of basic ingredients for the cake-maker. One tip for shopping is to buy size 3 eggs, which I find the most successful for baking. Eggs play such a critical role in cake-making, for lightening sponges and making them rise, so it is worth using the right size. If larger eggs are specifically required, then size 2 can be used.

TINS

It is an old rule of cake-making that time spent on preparing the tin is seldom wasted. Nothing is more disappointing than to damage the cake in attempting to get it out of an ill-prepared tin. I have used the excellent Prestige range of tins throughout this book, but whichever tins you use, make sure you follow the manufacturer's instructions. Never bake a cake in a brand new tin: bake off the shininess in a hot oven and allow to cool before preparing it and filling it with cake mixture.

Take the extra time to line the bottom of tins, a process which is made much easier if the tin itself is lightly greased first. Then, once cooked, do not rush to get the cake out of the tin. Quite apart from the risk of burning yourself, many cakes – sponges for instance – are liable to crack if handled too early. The richer the cake, the longer it should be left to cool, and a very rich cake should cool completely in the tin.

OVENS

More often than not, if the recipe method has been followed accurately, the major problems arise from the oven. Unfortunately, ovens vary enormously, and over long periods of cooking, even a small difference of a few degrees is magnified. As a rough guide, fan-assisted cooks more quickly than conventional, and electric is faster than gas. Unhelpful though it may sound, there is no substitute for knowing your own oven. I suggest that you buy a thermometer (I recommend the Brannan range), as this is the only way of ensuring pinpoint accuracy.

Finally, never forget the kitchen skewer, an absolutely vital item of equipment to keep beside your oven. If a skewer comes out clean from the middle of a cake, then it's cooked, but if it comes out with cake mixture on it, it needs more cooking. And when the cake is still cooking, apart from doing a fingertip or skewer test after the minimum cooking time, try not to succumb to curiosity by opening the oven door to inspect progress. Set the timer and don't take a look till the buzzer goes off.

STORAGE

For keeping them at their best, most cakes need storing in an airtight container in a cool, dry place. However, they vary enormously in their storability, ranging from fatless sponges which dry out rapidly, to fruit cakes which improve with time and should be allowed to mature to allow the flavours to mingle.

Cakes freeze surprisingly well, and can be left in the freezer for up to six months. Make sure the cake is completely cool, then place it in a freezer bag. While it is still soft, don't let it get pushed out of shape by other frozen food, and when defrosting, allow between 2-3 hours for sponges and overnight for big fruit cakes.

A useful tip for children's party cakes, when you are cutting out shapes for a character or an object, is to freeze the cake first. It is much simpler to work with a frozen, or at least chilled cake.

TRANSPORT

Moving cakes to a party or wedding can be a nightmare. It is essential to have either a deep box, tin or plastic container. Lift from the bottom not the sides and consider using the detachable top as the base for the cake, putting the main container over the body of the cake. I also recommend putting one sheet of strong paper under the cakeboard to enable you to get your fingers under the edge of the board. If you intend to travel by car, avoid the temptation to hold the box or container on your knees, it is much safer on the floor or in the boot, wedged in such a fashion as to ensure it cannot move.

CONVERSION TABLES

| WEIGHT | | SIZE | |
IMPERIAL	METRIC	IMPERIAL	METRIC
½oz	15g	4ins	10cm
1oz	28g	5ins	13cm
2oz	57g	6ins	16.5cm
3oz	85g	7ins	18cm
4oz	115g	8ins	20.5cm
5oz	145g	9ins	23cm
6oz	170g	10ins	25.5cm
7oz	200g	11ins	28cm
8oz	225g	12ins	30.5cm
9oz	255g	13ins	33cm
10oz	285g	14ins	35.5cm
11oz	315g	15ins	38cm
12oz	340g	16ins	40.5cm
13oz	370g		
14oz	397g		
15oz	425g		
16oz	445g		

MAKING BUTTERCREAM

Buttercream is also known as butter icing. It is made by creaming well sifted icing sugar with either soft margarine or unsalted butter. I suggest this is done by hand, but you can use a food mixer. The rule for buttercream is: the longer you beat the lighter it becomes, both in texture and colour. This is because the beating action introduces more air.

INGREDIENTS

Metric		Imperial
170g	Unsalted butter	6oz
341g	Sieved icing sugar	12oz
45ml	Warm water	3tbsp

All ingredients should be warmed to 65/70°F when making buttercream.

Soften butter and beat until light. Gradually add the sieved icing sugar, beating well after each addition.

Add and beat in the water.

Colour and flavour with chocolate, cocoa etc. if required.

SIMPLE SPONGE CAKE

INGREDIENTS

Metric		Imperial
	1 egg, size 3	
85g	Caster sugar	3oz
85g	Self raising flour, sifted	3oz
30ml	Hot water	2tbsp

BAKING TIN

20cm (8in) round sponge tin, greased and floured.

BAKING

Preheated oven, 200°C or 400°F or gas mark 6. When the sponge has been baking for 14 minutes, open the oven door slowly, and if the sponge is pale in colour continue baking. When it is golden brown, draw fingers across the top of it, lightly pressing, and if this leaves indentation, continue baking. Repeat test every 2-3 minutes until the top springs back when touched.

STORAGE

Wrap the cooled sponge in waxed paper and store in an airtight tin, eating it within 3 days. Or freeze for up to 6 months and use within 3 days of defrosting.

Mary's Tips

For a chocolate sponge, follow the same recipe but replace 14g (½oz) of flour with 14g (½oz) of cocoa powder

1. Using a pastry brush, grease tin(s) with white fat.

2. Sprinkle sufficient flour into sponge tin to cover base and side.

3. Gently shake and turn tin until all the grease is covered with flour. Then tap out excess flour.

4. Crack open an egg into a small basin before putting into the mixing bowl. Repeat for each egg (to ensure bad doesn't mix with good).

5. Lightly whisk egg.

6. Pour caster sugar into mixing bowl with the beaten egg.

7. Whisk briskly until thick and creamy.

8. Stir-in the hot water.

9. Sprinkle sieved flour on to the mixture.

10. Gently fold in flour with a spatula.

11. Transfer mixture to the prepared tin(s).

12. Place tin(s) near top of pre-heated oven (400°F, 200°C or Gas Mark 6).

13. At end of recommended baking time, test sponge in accordance with the instructions on page 6.

14. After baking, leave to cool for five minutes. Then remove from tin on to greaseproof paper covered in caster sugar.

15. Upturn sponge and place on wire tray until cold. (See instructions for storage on page 6.)

SIMPLE GENOESE CAKE

INGREDIENTS

Metric		Imperial
85g	Butter	3oz
85g	Margarine	3oz
170g	Caster sugar	6oz
	1 egg, size 3	
170g	Self raising flour, sifted	6oz

For a chocolate genoese, replace 28g (1oz) of flour with 28g (1oz) of cocoa powder.

BAKING TIN

Use either a 25.5cm (10in) round tin, or a 23cm (9in) square sponge tin, or a 25.5cm (10in) hoop tin.

BAKING

Preheated oven, 190°C or 375°F or gas mark 5, for 20 minutes. When the genoese has been baking for 20 minutes, open the oven door slowly, and if it is still pale, continue baking. When the genoese is golden brown, draw fingers across it, lightly pressing, and if this leaves an indentation, continue baking. Repeat test every 2-3 minutes until the top springs back when touched.

Mary's Tips

The French traditional small cakes – madeleines – baked in shell-shaped individual tins, are made with genoese mixture.

STORAGE

Wrap the cooled genoese in waxed paper and store in an airtight tin. Or freeze in the waxed paper for up to 6 months, and use within 3 days of defrosting.

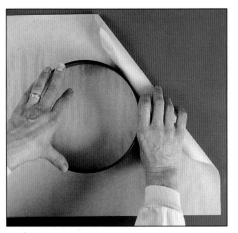

1. PREPARING A HOOP
Place a hoop on double sheet of greaseproof paper and roll one corner into side of hoop.

2. Continue rolling paper tightly around the base of the hoop.

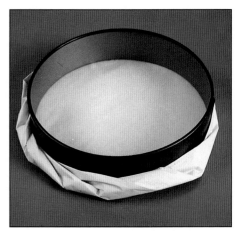

3. Tuck in the end of the paper to complete hoop base, then place on baking sheet. Grease inside of hoop and base lightly with white fat.

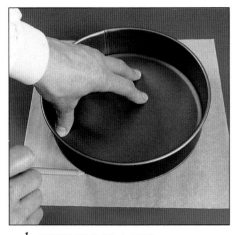

1. PREPARING A TIN
Using sponge tin, mark and then cut out a disc of greaseproof paper.

2. Using a pastry brush, grease tin(s) with white fat.

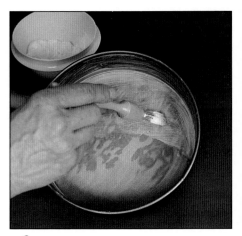

3. Place greaseproof paper disc into bottom of the tin and brush over with white fat.

1. MAKING A GENOESE
Mix then beat the margarine and butter until soft and light.

2. Beat in caster sugar to form a fluffy consistency. Crack open the egg in a separate bowl.

3. Thoroughly beat in a small portion of egg at a time until all egg is used.

4. Pour sieved flour on to mixture.

5. Gently fold flour into mixture. (Don't overmix.)

6. Spoon mixture into prepared hoop(s) or tin(s).

7. Evenly spread mixture with a spatula.

8. Place tin(s) at centre of pre-heated oven (375°F/190°C or Gas Mark 5).

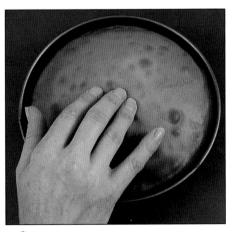

9. At end of recommended baking time, test genoese in accordance with the instructions at the top of page 8. After baking, see Nos. 14/15 on page 7.

MAKING A BASIC FRUIT CAKE

INGREDIENTS

Metric	for a 445g (1lb) cake	Imperial
57g	Plain flour	2oz
57g	Brown sugar	2oz
57g	Butter	2oz
71g	Currants	2½oz
71g	Sultanas	2½oz
28g	Seedless raisins	1oz
28g	Glacé cherries	1oz
42g	Mixed peel	1½oz
21g	Ground almonds	¾oz
2tsp	Brandy or rum	½fl. oz
	1 egg, size 2	
	1 pinch nutmeg	
	1 pinch mixed spice	
	1 pinch salt	
	Zest and juice from ¼ lemon	

SOAKING MIXTURE

Equal quantities of rum, sherry and glycerine, or spirits of your choice: 15ml (1tbsp) per 445g (1lb) of cake, to be brushed on to the cooked cake.

BAKING TIN

Use either a 13cm (5in) round tin, or a 10cm (4in) square tin, approximately 7.5cm (3in) deep, for this basic amount of ingredients. Multiply ingredients for larger cakes, and increase the size of the tin accordingly.

BAKING

Bake at 140°C or 275°F or gas mark 1 for 1¼ hours for a 1lb cake; 1¼ hrs for a 2lb cake; 2½ hrs for a 3lb cake; 3½ hrs for a 4lb cake; 4 hrs for a 5lb cake; 4¼ hrs for a 6lb cake.

At the end of the guide time for baking, test the cake to ensure it is cooked all through. Slide the cake in its tin to the front of the oven. Insert a steel skewer into the centre, slowly remove it, and if it is clean, the cake is ready. If mixture clings to the skewer, lift it out of the cake, slide back the tin and continue testing every 10 minutes.

STORAGE

Wrap the cooled cake in waxed paper – never in clingfilm, tinfoil or a sealed plastic container. Place on a cake board and store in a cool, dry atmosphere which allows odourless air circulation with no direct sunlight.

Although it isn't necessary to freeze this fruit cake, it can be done. But a decorated fruit cake should not be frozen unless the almond paste and icing has been removed first.

Mary's Tips

• Calculate the size of fruit cake you need by using a guide of 8 generous portions from each 445g (1lb) of finished, iced cake.

• A darker fruit cake can be made by substituting 10% of the brown sugar with black treacle.

• If not stored correctly, the cake could become mouldy for various reasons:

– being wrapped while still warm;

– being wrapped after out for too long;

– wrapping it in inferior-quality paper;

– being stored in a variable temperature;

– under-baking;

– too much soaking with alcohol after baking;

– being stored in a damp atmosphere.

• Too hot an oven will produce a cracked crusted top and an uncooked centre. In addition the fruit may be burnt and bitter.

• Too cool an oven will produce uncooked fruit which will dry out quickly and have a very thick crust.

• If the cake has been baked in the correct temperature but the middle sinks, it could be there was too much: liquid in the batter, baking powder, sugar, or fat.

• If the baked cake is crumbly, any of the following could be the cause: curdled batter, overbeaten fat, sugar and eggs, undermixing the flour and fruit, or too little sugar.

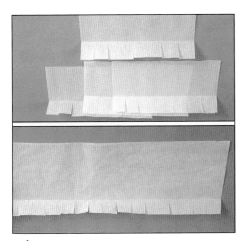

1. Cut greaseproof paper 5cm (2") deeper than cake-tin to cover side(s). (4 pieces for square tin and 1 piece for round tin.)

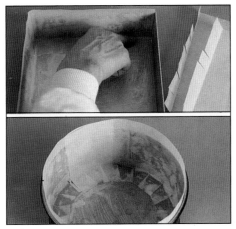

2. Grease tin then cover side(s) and 2.5cm (1") around base with the prepared greaseproof paper. Also ensure paper is 2.5cm (1") above tin height.

3. Cut greaseproof paper and fit into base of tin, then grease with butter or margarine.

4. Weigh ingredients out onto separate sheets of greaseproof paper, using recipe on page 10, multiplying the ingredients if necessary.

5. Inspect, wash and dry fruit and then chop cherries in half.

6. Grate the lemon and put the zest with the fruit and liquor into a bowl and thoroughly mix.

7. Thoroughly mix and sieve flour, salt and spices on to greaseproof paper several times.

8. Crack open an egg into a small basin before putting into the mixing bowl. Repeat for each egg (to ensure bad doesn't mix with good).

9. Leave all ingredients at room temperature for 12 hours (65°F or 18°C).

10. *Beat butter until light.*

11. *Add and beat in sugar until light.*

12. *Thoroughly beat in a small portion of egg at a time until all egg is used.*

13. *Stir in the ground almonds.*

14. *Add flour and spices to mixture.*

15. *Fold flour and spices lightly into mixture and mix until clear.*

16. *Add fruit and liquor.*

17. *Add lemon juice to mixture.*

18. *Stir mixture thoroughly, but* **DO NOT BEAT**.

19. *Spoon required quantity of mixture into prepared cake tin(s).*

20. *Dip hand in luke warm water and then flatten mixture with the back of wet hand.*

21. *Place cake-tin in centre of pre-heated oven (275°F, 140°C or Gas Mark 1) – with ovenproof bowl containing water beneath.*

22. *At half the baking time, remove water from oven.*

23. *At end of recommended baking time test cake in accordance with instructions on page 10.*

24. *When cake is baked, remove from oven and leave in cool place for 24 hours in the tin.*

25. *Prepare soaking mixture (see page 10).*

26. *Carefully remove greaseproof paper from cake. Upturn cake and brush on soaking mixture (one tablespoon per pound of cake).*

27. *Wrap cake in waxed paper, date it and store cake to mature. (See page 10 for storage instructions.)*

CITRUS CAKE

Serves 8

CHANTILLY GOLD

Mary's Tips

Lemon, orange or lime curd can be used as an alternative.

Double the recipe and divide into three 445g (1lb) loaf tins.

Improves with freezing.

INGREDIENTS

Metric		Imperial
115g	Soft margarine	4oz
100g	Caster sugar	3½oz
	2 eggs, size 2	
30ml	Lemon curd	2tbsp
145g	Self raising flour, sifted	5oz

TOPPING SYRUP

30ml	Granulated sugar dissolved in juice of ½ a lemon.	2tbsp

BAKING TIN

905g (2lb) loaf tin greased and base lined.

BAKING

Preheated oven, 180°C or 360°F or gas mark 4
Middle shelf
50-55 minutes

1. Place all the ingredients into a mixing bowl. Beat until light and fluffy. Do not overbeat.

2. Spoon the mixture into the base lined loaf tin. Place into preheated oven on middle shelf and bake.

3. When baked immediately brush the cake with the topping syrup. Leave cake in tin until cool. Remove from tin and place onto a wire tray until cold.

RHUBARB and DATE CAKE

Serves 12

RAFFLES

1. Sift the flour and baking powder into a bowl. Rub in the margarine to form a fine crumbly texture. Stir in the sugar.

INGREDIENTS

Metric		Imperial
170g	Plain flour	6oz
2.5ml	Baking powder	½tsp
85g	Margarine	3oz
115g	Caster sugar	4oz
225g	Rhubarb	8oz
115g	Stoned dates, chopped	4oz
	1 egg, size 3, beaten	
60ml	Milk	4tbsp

BAKING TIN

16.5cm (6½in) round cake tin greased and lined with greaseproof paper.

BAKING

Preheated oven, 190°C or 370°F or gas mark 5
Middle shelf
1½-2 hours

2. Wipe the rhubarb and cut into small cubes. Stir the rhubarb and dates into the mixture.

Mary's Tips

Pale pink forced rhubarb has a mellower flavour than the robust outdoor variety, but both work well with the sweetness of dates.

3. Stir in the beaten egg and milk. Place into the tin, level and bake. After baking leave 10 minutes then turn out onto a wire tray to cool. Dust with icing sugar.

15

PEAR and APRICOT CAKE

Serves 8-12

Mary's Tips

Vary the flavour of the filling by using lemon, fruit liqueur or cherry jam.

Sieve icing sugar. However fine, the tiniest lumps can result in roughness. "The longest way round is the shortest way home."

INGREDIENTS

Metric		Imperial
170g	Butter or margarine	6oz
170g	Caster sugar	6oz
	3 eggs, size 2, beaten	
170g	Self raising flour	6oz
57g	Dried pears, chopped	2oz
57g	Dried apricots, chopped	2oz
28g	Glacé cherries, chopped	1oz
28g	Angelica, chopped	1oz

FILLING

57g	Butter	2oz
115g	Icing sugar, sifted	4oz
10ml	Kirsch	2tsp
	1 egg yolk	

BAKING TINS

Two 18.5cm (7¼in) square sandwich tins greased and lined.

BAKING

Preheated oven, 180°C or 360°F or gas mark 4
Middle shelf
25 minutes or until golden brown

1. Cream the butter and sugar until light and fluffy. Then beat in the egg, a little at a time.

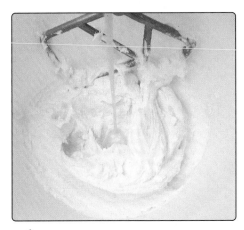

2. Sift the flour over the mixture and fold in lightly, with a metal spoon.

3. Mix in the chopped pears and apricots. Divide the mixture equally between the two sandwich tins.

4. Scatter the chopped cherries and angelica over the mixture in one tin. Bake the cakes then turn out onto a wire tray until cold.

5. For the filling, beat the butter and icing sugar until soft and creamy. Add the kirsch and egg yolk and beat until pale in colour.

6. Sandwich the sponges together with the filling, then sprinkle the top lightly with caster sugar.

CARROT CAKE (PASSION CAKE)

Serves 12-16

WORCESTER HERBS

1. Mix together the grated carrot, oil, sugar, whisked eggs, syrup and vanilla essence until smooth.

2. Sift together the flour, bicarbonate of soda, baking powder, cinnamon, grated nutmeg and salt. Then mix in the chopped walnuts and bran.

INGREDIENTS

Metric		Imperial
225g	Carrots, grated	8oz
170ml	Corn oil	6floz
170g	Light brown soft sugar	6oz
	3 eggs, size 3, whisked	
30ml	Golden syrup	2tbsp
5ml	Vanilla essence	1tsp
170g	Plain flour	6oz
5ml	Bicarbonate of soda	1tsp
5ml	Baking powder	1tsp
5ml	Cinnamon	1tsp
2.5ml	Grated nutmeg	½tsp
5ml	Salt	1tsp
115g	Walnut pieces, roughly chopped	4oz
28g	Bran	1oz

FILLING AND TOPPING

Metric		Imperial
115g	Butter	4oz
225g	Icing sugar, sifted	8oz
115g	Philadelphia cream cheese or low fat soft cheese	4oz
2.5ml	Vanilla essence	½tsp

DECORATION

Whole pecan nuts
Sugarpaste carrots

BAKING TIN

21.5cm (8½in) round cake tin lined with greaseproof paper and greased.

BAKING

Preheated oven, 180°C or 360°F or gas mark 4
Middle shelf
1¼ hours

Mary's Tips

Cold eggs can cause mixtures to curdle. Before use, place whole eggs in hand-hot water for about 5 minutes to allow them to warm through.

3. Stir in the carrot mixture then beat well. Pour mixture into the tin and bake. After baking leave in tin for 5 minutes then turn out onto a wire tray until cold.

4. For the filling, cream the butter and icing sugar until smooth. Beat in the cheese and essence until light and fluffy.

5. Cut and fill the centre, then coat the top, using a combed scraper or fork. Decorate with pecan nuts and sugarpaste carrots.

GOLDEN BRAN CAKE

Serves 10-12

INGREDIENTS

Mary's Tips

Cut into thin slices and spread lightly with butter for best eating results.

Eat within 5 days.

Freezes.

Metric		Imperial
170g	Self raising flour	6oz
85g	Butter or margarine	3oz
57g	Natural bran	2oz
85g	Light brown soft sugar	3oz
5ml	Mixed spice	1tsp
	2 eggs, size 2, beaten	
30ml	Golden syrup	2 level tbsp
85g	Sultanas	3oz
150ml	Milk, approximately	¼pt

BAKING TIN

905g (2lb) loaf tin greased and base lined.

BAKING

Preheated oven, 180°C or 360°F or gas mark 4
Middle shelf
60 minutes or until firm when pressed in the centre. Leave in the tin to cool, before placing on a wire tray.

1. Sift the flour into a bowl, then rub in the butter or margarine. Stir in the bran, sugar and spice.

2. Add the eggs, syrup and sultanas with sufficient milk to form a fairly soft mixture.

3. Place mixture into the tin and sprinkle the top with a light layer of bran. Bake.

CHERRY and ALMOND CAKE

Serves 10-12

1. Cut cherries in half, wash and drain, leave to dry on a tea-towel overnight. Sift flours together into a bowl then mix in the ground almonds and cherries.

2. Beat the margarine, butter and sugar together until light and fluffy. Beat in the eggs a little at a time. Blend the mixtures together, using a spoon.

3. Spoon mixture into tin, and spread chopped cherries and almonds on top. When baked leave in tin for 10 minutes then place cake on a wire tray until cold.

INGREDIENTS

Metric		Imperial
225g	Glacé cherries	8oz
145g	Self raising flour	5oz
57g	Plain flour	2oz
35g	Cornflour	1¼oz
35g	Ground almonds	1¼oz
85g	Margarine	3oz
85g	Butter	3oz
170g	Caster sugar	6oz
	3 eggs, size 3	

TOPPING

28g	Flaked almonds	1oz
28g	Cherries, chopped and washed	1oz

BAKING TIN

16.5cm (6½in) round cake tin greased and lined with greaseproof paper and lightly greased.

BAKING

Preheated oven, 180°C or 360°F or gas mark 4
Middle shelf
1-1½ hours

Mary's Tips

Glacé cherries often come in an over-sticky, sweet syrup, which is the reason they need washing and drying before use.

ALL-IN-ONE SWISS ROLL

Serves 10-12

LAVINIA

1. Place all the ingredients into a bowl and beat until light and creamy.

2. Pour the mixture into the tin and spread evenly, using a trowel shaped palette knife and bake.

3. Place a moist tea-towel onto table, then greaseproof paper on top covered with caster sugar. When baked turn out sponge immediately onto sugared paper.

INGREDIENTS

Metric		Imperial
85g	Soft margarine	3oz
170g	Caster sugar	6oz
	3 eggs, size 2	
170g	Self raising flour	6oz
	FILLING	
57g	Jam, warmed	2oz

BAKING TIN

33 x 23cm (13 x 9in) swiss roll tin, greased and lined with greaseproof paper, then greased.

BAKING

Preheated oven, 200°C or 390°F or gas mark 6
Middle shelf
10-12 minutes

Mary's Tips

The classic all-in-one swiss roll is quick and easy to make once the technique of rolling the hot sponge is mastered.

Swiss roll is often made with butter. If you do not intend to eat it all on the first day butter helps to keep it moister for longer.

Waste no time once the sponge is cooked. If you are slow the edges will go crisp as they cool – making the sponge crack as you roll.

The following variations suggest combinations of flavours, fillings and coatings.

1. CHOCOLATE ROLL

Substitute 30ml (2tbsp) of flour with 30ml (2tbsp) of cocoa powder, and follow the same recipe and method as below. Fill the roll with chocolate buttercream, whipped cream or ice-cream just before serving.

2. GINGER CREAM ROLL

Make according to basic recipe, but fill it with 300ml (½pt) whipped double cream mixed with 45ml (3tbsp) ginger wine and 30ml (2tbs) finely chopped crystallised ginger. Use the excess to cover the outside of the roll and decorate with crystallised ginger.

3. WALNUT AND ORANGE ROLL

Make according to basic recipe, but add the grated rind of one orange to the mixture. Cook and leave to cool, rolled up, then finely chop 115g (4oz) walnuts. Beat 15-30ml (1-2tbsp) of honey into 115g (4oz) soft cheese. Stir in the nuts and fill the cake with the mixture.

4. Remove the greaseproof paper the sponge was baked in, then immediately roll up the sponge and leave for 5 minutes to cool.

5. Carefully unroll the sponge and spread the filling evenly on top.

6. Roll up again, without the sugared paper or towel, and leave to cool on a wire tray.

ORANGE SEED CAKE

Serves 12-16

SANDRINGHAM

1. Cream the margarine until soft. Add the sugar and beat until light and fluffy. Thoroughly beat in the eggs, one at a time.

2. Stir in the seeds, milk and orange rind. Sift together the flour and baking powder and fold into the creamed mixture, alternately with orange juice.

3. Spoon the mixture into the prepared mould and bake. After baking leave to cool for 5 minutes then turn out onto a wire tray to cool. Dust with icing sugar.

INGREDIENTS

Metric		Imperial
170g	Block margarine	6oz
170g	Caster sugar	6oz
	3 eggs, size 3	
15ml	Caraway seeds	1tbsp
15ml	Milk	1tbsp
	Grated rind and juice of 1 orange	
225g	Plain flour	8oz
7.5ml	Baking powder	1½ level tsp
	Icing sugar for decoration	

BAKING TIN

21.5cm (8½in) brioche tin, well greased.

BAKING

Preheated oven, 170°C or 340°F or gas mark 4
Middle shelf
45 minutes

24

BUTTERMILK CHEESECAKE

Serves 16

1. BASE. Mix the crumbled biscuits and sugar together then blend in the melted butter. Press mixture into the tin to cover base and a little up the side.

2. FILLING. Mix the egg, sugar and essence together then beat into the cream cheese. Stir in cream and buttermilk to make mixture a thick batter consistency.

ROYAL GARDEN

3. Fold in the melted butter. Pour mixture into tin and bake. After baking leave in tin until cold. Chill before removing from tin, decorate and serve.

INGREDIENTS

Metric		Imperial
	BASE	
	8 digestive biscuits, crumbled	
15ml	Light brown soft sugar	1tbsp
57g	Butter, melted	2oz
	FILLING	
	3 eggs, size 3, lightly beaten	
170g	Caster sugar	6oz
5ml	Vanilla essence	1tsp
680g	Cream cheese	1½lb
225ml	Sour cream	8oz
225ml	Buttermilk	8oz
57g	Butter	2oz

BAKING TIN

21.5cm (8½in) round loose-bottomed cake tin, base lined.

BAKING

Preheated oven, 160°C or 320°F or gas mark 2½
Middle shelf
45-60 minutes

DECORATION

Fresh cream, whipped
Fresh fruit

LEMON and CHOCOLATE LAYER CAKE

Serves 8-10

SUMMERFIELD

1. Sift together the flour, salt and baking powder. Rub in the margarine.

2. Add the sugar, egg, lemon rind and milk.

3. Stir the mixture with a wooden spoon until a soft dropping consistency is reached.

4. Spoon one third of the mixture into the tin, then sprinkle on some of the grated chocolate, as shown.

INGREDIENTS

Metric		Imperial
340g	Plain flour	12oz
	Pinch of salt	
15ml	Baking powder	1tsp
130g	Margarine	4½oz
130g	Caster sugar	4½oz
	2 eggs, size 4	
	Grated lemon rind	3tsp
2ml	Milk	7oz
170g	Plain chocolate or cooking chocolate, finely chopped or grated	6oz

TOPPING

Icing sugar

BAKING TIN

16.5cm (6in) round cake tin greased and base lined with greased greaseproof paper.

BAKING

Preheated oven, 190°C or 370°F or gas mark 5 for 15 minutes, then reduce heat to 180°C or 350°F or gas mark 4 for one hour. Middle shelf.

5. Spoon half the remaining mixture on top, then add more grated chocolate.

Mary's Tips

Plain chocolate gives a better taste than cooking chocolate in this recipe. Real chocolate chips are now widely available for cake-making and can be chopped more finely, rather than grating a block.

Salt is a key ingredient in this, as in many other recipes. Without it, cakes can be flavourless. It also makes the gluten in the flour more elastic, thereby helping the mixture to rise.

6. Spoon remaining mixture on top then, finally, sprinkle on the remaining grated chocolate.

7. Bake as recommended. When baked, leave in the tin for 30 minutes. Then remove from tin and leave to cool on a wire tray.

8. Using a fine sieve, dust the top lightly with icing sugar.

SIMNEL CAKE

Serves 16

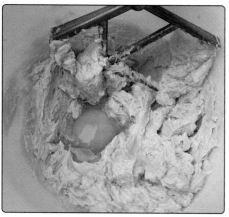

1. Cream the butter and sugar together until light and fluffy. Thoroughly beat in the eggs, one at a time.

2. Mix the remaining dry ingredients together, then fold into the creamed butter, adding milk to make soft mixture. Spoon half the mixture into the tin.

3. Roll out the almond paste and place into the tin, then fill with remaining mixture. Slightly hollow the top. After baking leave in the tin for 30 minutes.

INGREDIENTS

Metric		Imperial
225g	Plain wholemeal flour	8oz
170g	Light brown soft sugar	6oz
170g	Butter	6oz
	3 eggs, size 3	
170g	Sultanas	6oz
115g	Currants	4oz
57g	Peel	2oz
57g	Cherries	2oz
2.5ml	Mixed spice	½tsp
1.25ml	Cinnamon	¼tsp
57g	Ground almonds	2oz
	Grated rind of 1 lemon	
	Grated rind of 1 small orange	
	Milk as required	

CAKE CENTRE

115g	Almond paste or marzipan	4oz

TOP DECORATION

Boiled apricot jam
340g (12oz) almond paste or marzipan
85g (3oz) sugarpaste
Royal icing for piping
Various food colours

GUM ARABIC SOLUTION

45ml (1½oz) water
15g (½oz) gum arabic powder
Boil the water, remove from heat and whisk in the powder. Leave to cool.

BAKING TIN

16.5cm (6in) round cake tin greased and lined with greaseproof paper.

BAKING

Preheated oven, 160°C or 320°F or gas mark 2½ for 1 hour then reduce heat to 150°C or 300°F or gas mark 2 for further 2-2½ hours Middle shelf

4. Remove baking paper and place cake onto a wire tray until cold. Brush top with boiling apricot jam. Mould almond paste balls and place around cake edge.

5. Make gum arabic solution. Place cake under a grill to colour the almond paste. Then immediately brush almond paste with gum arabic solution.

6. When the cake is cold, roll out the sugarpaste and cut into a fluted disc and place onto the cake-top.

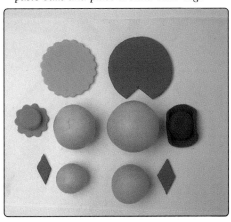

7. Mould the various chicken shapes shown from sugarpaste or almond paste.

8. Fix the pieces together and decorate with piping and bows.

9. Fix the chickens and then pipe appropriate inscription.

ALL-IN-ONE VICTORIA SANDWICH CAKE

Serves 12

ENGLISH GARDEN

MAYFIELD

Mary's Tips

A few drops of vanilla essence can be added for a different taste.

FILLING

Raspberry jam
Buttercream (see p.5)

INGREDIENTS

Metric		Imperial
285g	Self raising flour	10oz
12.5ml	Baking powder	2½tsp
285g	Margarine	10oz
285g	Caster sugar	10oz
	5 eggs, size 3	

TOPPING

Icing sugar

BAKING TINS

Two 21.5cm (8½in) round sandwich tins greased and floured.

BAKING

Preheated oven, 170°C or 340°F or gas mark 3
Middle shelf
35-45 minutes

1. Thoroughly sift the self raising flour and baking powder together, then place all the ingredients into a bowl.

2. Beat on slow speed, or by hand with a wooden spoon, until well mixed.

3. Divide the mixture equally into the tins and gently spread level. Bake. Turn out onto a wire tray to cool. Sandwich together then dust top with icing sugar.

GOLDEN SYRUP CAKE

Serves 8-10

Mary's Tips

This cake freezes particularly well, but don't sprinkle it with the demerara sugar until it is defrosted. Eat within 3 days if fresh, or after defrosting.

INGREDIENTS

Metric		Imperial
225g	Margarine	8oz
115g	Demerara sugar	4oz
115ml	Golden syrup	4oz
	4 eggs, size 2	
225g	Self raising flour	8oz
	TOPPING	
15g	Demerara sugar	½oz

BAKING TIN

16cm (6¼in) round cake tin greased and base lined.

BAKING

Preheated oven, 180°C or 360°F or gas mark 4
Middle shelf
55 minutes or until cooked

1. Cream the margarine, sugar and syrup together until light and fluffy.

2. Thoroughly beat in the egg, a little at a time. Sift and gently fold in the flour.

3. Spoon mixture into the tin. Bake. When baked leave for 10 minutes. Turn out onto a wire tray. Sprinkle top with demerara sugar.

UNCOOKED CHOCOLATE CAKE

Serves 16-20

1. Roughly crush biscuits, then chop walnuts and mix together. Cream butter, sugar and syrup together. Beat in cocoa then mix in the biscuits.

INGREDIENTS

Metric		Imperial
115g	Sweet biscuits	4oz
57g	Digestive biscuits	2oz
57g	Walnuts	2oz
100g	Butter or margarine	3½oz
28g	Caster sugar	1oz
85g	Golden syrup	3oz
57g	Cocoa powder, sifted	2oz
	TOPPING	
115ml	Milk chocolate	4oz
15ml	Hot water	1tbsp
57g	Butter	2oz
170g	Icing sugar, sifted	6oz

CAKE TIN

Grease a 20.5cm (8in) flan ring and place onto a flat serving dish or board.

TO MAKE THE TOPPING

Slowly heat the chocolate, water and butter together in a saucepan until all melted. Then beat in the icing sugar.

2. Press evenly into the flan ring. Cover and leave overnight in a refrigerator.

Mary's Tips

A mixture of dark and white chocolate, grated, with whole walnuts round the edge, makes very effective decoration

3. After cooling cake overnight make the topping and spread over top, using a fork. Fix walnuts around the edge and sprinkle chocolate over the centre.

COCONUT CAKE

Serves 10-14

WORCESTER HERBS

INGREDIENTS

Metric		Imperial
145g	Butter or margarine	5oz
170g	Caster sugar	6oz
	2 eggs, size 2	
45ml	Milk	3tbsp
225g	Self raising flour, sifted	8oz
115g	Dessicated coconut	4oz

TOPPING

115g	Philadelphia cheese	4oz
28g	Butter	1oz
170g	Icing sugar, sifted	6oz

DECORATION

Toasted flaked coconut

BAKING TIN

905g (2lb) loaf tin greased and base lined.

BAKING

Preheated oven, 170°C or 340°F or gas mark 3
Middle shelf
1½ hours.

1. Cream the butter and sugar until light and fluffy. Beat together the egg and milk. Add slowly to the creamed butter and sugar, beating well.

2. Slowly fold in the flour and coconut, using a metal spoon, until clear. Spoon mixture into tin and bake. After baking remove from tin when cold.

3. Beat all the ingredients for the topping together, until pale and creamy in colour. Then pipe onto the cake-top. Sprinkle with toasted coconut.

AUSTRIAN COFFEE CAKE
Serves 16-20

VICEROY GOLD

34

INGREDIENTS

Metric		Imperial
255g	Butter	9oz
225g	Caster sugar	8oz
	4 eggs, size 2, separated	
5ml	Grated lemon rind	1tsp
28g	Vanilla sugar	1oz
285g	Plain flour	10oz
5ml	Baking powder	1tsp

SOAKING MIXTURE

255g (9oz) strong black coffee, cold
Soft light brown sugar to taste
Brandy to taste

COATING

285g (10oz) whipping cream
Coffee flavouring
85g (3oz) toasted flaked almonds
Coffee powder for dusting

BAKING TIN

21.5cm (8½in) round cake tin greased and fully lined.

BAKING

Preheated oven, 180℃ or 360°F or gas mark 4
Middle shelf
1¼ hours

1. Beat together the butter and caster sugar until light and fluffy. Thoroughly beat in the egg yolks, one at a time. Then mix in the grated lemon rind.

2. Sift the flour and baking powder together. Whisk the egg whites with the vanilla sugar until stiff.

3. Lightly fold into the creamed butter, alternate spoonfuls of egg white and flour until well blended. Place in tin and bake. When baked, leave in tin for 10 minutes.

4. Turn out onto a wire tray to cool. Mix cold coffee with sugar and brandy to taste. Place cake back into tin, prick top with skewer and brush on liquid.

5. Leave to soak for 2 hours. Whip the cream and flavour with coffee. Remove cake from tin and coat top and side with the cream.

6. Sprinkle toasted flaked almonds onto the cake top then cover the sides. Dust the top with cocoa powder. Chill and serve.

CHOCOLATE and ORANGE CAKE

Serves 8-10

1. *Beat the butter and sugar until light and fluffy. Then mix in the grated orange and lemon rind.*

2. *Stir in the chocolate powder and ground almonds then beat well again. Whisk the eggs in a separate bowl until well mixed.*

3. *Beat the eggs into the mixture a little at a time, add a tablespoon of the flour and the brandy if required. Fold in remaining flour using a spatula, or spoon.*

INGREDIENTS

Metric		Imperial
115g	Butter	**4oz**
115g	Caster sugar	**4oz**
	Grated rind of ½ an orange	
	Grated rind of ½ a lemon	
57g	Drinking chocolate powder	**2oz**
115g	Ground almonds	**4oz**
	2 eggs, size 2	
57g	Self raising flour, sifted	**2oz**
10ml	Brandy – optional	**1dsp**

SUGGESTED FILLINGS

Apricot jam
Orange or lemon curd
Raspberry jam

CHOCOLATE FUDGE ICING

115g (4oz) plain or milk chocolate
57g (2oz) unsalted butter
1 egg, size 3, beaten
170g (6oz) icing sugar, sifted

Mary's Tips

Variations on chocolate fudge icing include:

- adding finely chopped walnuts

- adding 30ml (2tbsp) rum

- adding grated orange rind

- using 15ml (1tbsp) honey instead of 25g (1oz) of sugar

- adding 5ml (1tsp) of instant coffee granules

- adding a pinch of ground ginger plus 30ml (2tbsp) of chopped stem ginger

905g (2lb) loaf tin, greased and base lined.

Preheated oven, 160°C or 320°F or gas mark 2½
Middle shelf
¾-1 hour

4. Spoon mixture into tin and bake. After baking leave for 20 minutes then turn out onto a wire tray to cool. Slice and fill, then coat with boiled apricot jam.

5. For topping, melt the chocolate and butter together, then stir in the beaten egg. Remove from heat, then stir in the icing sugar and beat well.

6. When topping is slightly cooled, spread over the cake-top and sides. Pipe remaining topping as shown then decorate as required.

CARAMEL SANDWICH CAKE

Serves 8

BEAUFORT

INGREDIENTS

Metric		Imperial
115g	Butter or margarine	4oz
115g	Granulated sugar	4oz
	2 eggs, size 3	
57g	Loaf sugar	2oz
150ml	Hot milk	¼pt
170g	Self-raising flour, sifted	6oz
2.5ml	Baking powder	½tsp
	Apricot jam	
	Icing sugar	

BAKING TIN

Two 19cm (7½in) round sandwich tins, greased and floured.

BAKING

Preheated oven, 190°C or 375°F or gas mark 5 for about 30 minutes.

Mary's Tips

When making caramel, allow the sugar to dissolve slowly over a gentle heat, without stirring, until it has turned brown.

1. Cream together the butter or margarine and the sugar until light. Separate eggs, and beat in the yolks.

2. Make a caramel by heating the loaf sugar in a small pan until it melts and turns light brown. Cool slightly.

3. Add the hot milk carefully and stir until the caramel is dissolved.

4. When caramel mixture is lukewarm, add it gradually to the creamed ingredients, and beat together.

5. Stir in the sieved dry ingredients and mix well, adding a little more milk if necessary. The mixture should be of soft dropping consistency.

6. Stiffly beat the egg whites and fold them in. Place in tins and bake as above. Fill the cooled cake with apricot jam and sprinkle the top with icing sugar.

INGREDIENTS

Metric		Imperial
	4 eggs, size 3	
115g	Caster sugar	4oz
115g	Plain flour	4oz
	few drops of almond essence	
31g	Melted butter	1¼oz
	FILLING	
300ml	Double cream	10fl.oz
30ml	Amaretto liqueur	2tbsp
	1 small can mandarin oranges	
	2 kiwi fruit, sliced	

BAKING TIN

32.5cm x 23cm (13 x 9in) swiss roll tin, greased and lined with greased greaseproof paper.

BAKING

Preheated oven at 200°C or 400°F or gas mark 6, for 8-10 minutes.

Mary's Tips

Any fruit can be combined with cream for a filling, according to taste and season.

Freeze by rolling up the warm swiss roll with paper inside. Wrap in waxed paper when cool, then freeze for up to 6 months.

Fill with cream and fruit when fully defrosted.

1. Whisk the eggs, sugar and almond essence over a pan of hot water. Beat until mixture is light, creamy, double in bulk and shows the marks of the beaters.

2. Fold in the sifted flour carefully, and fold in the melted butter gently.

3. Pour into the prepared swiss roll tin and bake for 8-10 minutes.

4. Turn out onto a sheet of greaseproof paper sprinkled with caster sugar. Remove the paper which lined the tin.

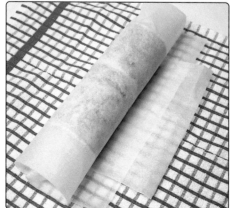

5. Lay a fresh piece of greaseproof paper on top, and carefully roll up the cake with the paper inside. Leave to cool.

6. For the filling, whisk the cream and liqueur to soft peaks, then fold in the chopped fruit, leaving a few pieces to decorate.

SWISS FRUIT ROLL

Serves 8

7. *Carefully unroll the cake, remove the paper, and spread evenly with the cream and fruit.*

8. *Roll up the cake again, and either sprinkle with caster sugar, or cover with more cream or butter icing, according to taste.*

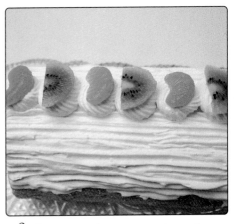

9. *Decorate with remaining pieces of fruit.*

SAFFRON CAKE

Serves 10-12

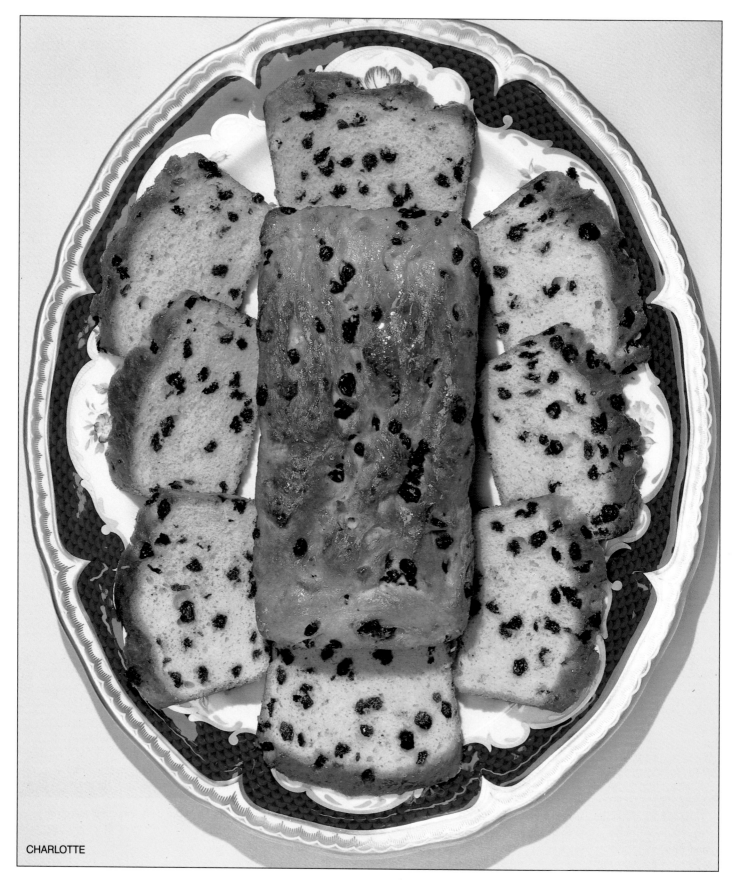

CHARLOTTE

INGREDIENTS

Metric		Imperial
150ml	Water	¼pt
	Pinch of saffron strands	
150ml	Milk	¼pt
15g	Dried yeast	½oz
	Pinch of sugar	
445g	Plain flour	1lb
5ml	Salt	1tsp
115g	Butter	4oz
170g	Currants	6oz
	Grated rind of ½ a lemon	
28g	Caster sugar	1oz

BAKING TINS

Two 905g (2lb) loaf tins greased and base lined.

BAKING

Preheated oven, 200°C or 390°F or gas mark 6 for 15 minutes then reduce heat to 180°C or 360°F or gas mark 4 for further 15-20 minutes
Middle shelf
Do not open the door during the baking.

Mary's Tips

This is a variation of the traditional Cornish saffron bread, which like this, is a rich golden-yellow colour from the saffron strands.

1. Boil the water, add saffron, remove heat and soak overnight. Warm the milk, add yeast and pinch of sugar, leave in a warm place for 15 minutes until frothy.

2. Sift the flour and salt together. Rub in the butter to form crumbly mixture then add the currants, grated rind and sugar.

3. Strain the saffron liquid into a saucepan and discard the strands. Warm slightly then mix into the dry ingredients.

4. Add the milk and yeast mixture and beat well to form a dough.

5. Divide the mixture between the two tins, cover with a cloth and leave in a warm place for 1 hour.

6. After 1 hour, or when the mixture has risen to ⅔rds the height of the tin, bake in the oven. When baked remove from tin and leave to cool on a wire tray.

DUNDEE CAKE

Serves 8-10

1. Dissolve the bicarbonate of soda in the water, pour into a saucepan and add the butter, sugar and fruits. Bring to boil on low heat then simmer for 15 minutes.

2. Remove from heat and leave to cool completely. Add the rum. Beat the eggs until frothy then add to the mixture.

3. Sift the flour and baking powder together then fold into the mixture with the syrup and marmalade, using a metal spoon.

INGREDIENTS

Metric		Imperial
5ml	Bicarbonate of soda	1tsp
60ml	Water	2fl.oz
115g	Butter or margarine	4oz
200g	Caster sugar	7oz
115g	Dried apricots, chopped	4oz
370g	Sultanas	13oz
60ml	Dark rum	4tbsp
	2 eggs, size 2	
225g	Strong plain flour, sifted	8oz
10ml	Baking powder	2tsp
15ml	Golden syrup	1tbsp
15ml	Marmalade	1 heated tbsp

TOPPING

57g	Blanched almonds, split in half	2oz
30ml	Milk	2tbsp
57g	Caster sugar	1oz

BAKING TIN

16.5cm (6½in) round cake tin greased and lined.

BAKING

Preheated oven, 170°C or 340°F or gas mark 3
Middle shelf
1¼ hours

BAKING TEST

Test cake with a skewer after 1¼ hours, if uncooked at this time reduce heat to 150°C or 300°F or gas mark 2 and cook until baked. When cooked, cool in the tin for 15 minutes, then turn out and leave to cool on a wire tray.

Mary's Tips

If you prefer the topping almonds not too brown, then remove the cake from the oven half way through and scatter them on, brushing with milk and sugar immediately. They will be less neatly arranged, but paler in colour on the finished cake.

The Dundee Cake is one of the most difficult to test for readiness. I recommend sticking the skewer down between the cake and the tin to warm the skewer. A warm skewer will give a better indication once it is stuck into the centre of the cake. If the skewer comes out quite clean – the cake is ready. If not, test after a further 10-15 minutes.

4. Place the almonds into a small bowl and cover with the milk. Leave for two minutes.

5. Spoon the cake mixture into the tin and level.

6. From the centre place the drained almonds in tight circles around cake-top. Sprinkle the top with milk then with caster sugar. Bake as recommended.

DATE and SPICE CAKE

Serves 8-10

1. Beat the butter until soft, then add the sugar and beat mixture until light and fluffy. Add the eggs, one at a time, beating well between each addition.

2. Sift together the flour, salt, baking powder and mixed spice into a bowl. Stir two tablespoons of this mixture into the dates.

3. Using a metal spoon, blend all ingredients together into the creamed mixture. Place into the tin, slightly hollow out the centre and bake.

INGREDIENTS

Metric		Imperial
225g	Butter	8oz
225g	Caster sugar	8oz
	3 eggs, size 2	
225g	Sugar rolled chopped dates	8oz
285g	Plain flour	10oz
2.5ml	Baking powder	1 level tsp
	Pinch of salt	
5ml	Mixed spice	2 level tsp

BAKING TIN

25.5cm (10in) round fluted cake tin, well greased and base lined.

BAKING

Preheated oven, 180°C or 360°F or gas mark 4 for 30 minutes then reduce to 160°C or 320°F or gas mark 3 for approximately 1½ hours. When baked leave in the tin for 30 minutes then turn out onto a wire tray.

Mary's Tips

This can also be made in a 20cm (8in) round tin or an 18cm (7in) square tin, greased and lined.

PINEAPPLE UPSIDE-DOWN CAKE

Serves 8-12

POPPIES

1. Brush the syrup over the greaseproof paper in the tin, then sprinkle on the brown sugar. Strain the pineapple rings and place the rings in the tin.

2. Whisk the eggs and sugar until light and fluffy. Sift the flour and gently fold into the mixture. Pour mixture into tin and bake.

3. After baking leave in the tin for 15 minutes, upturn and carefully turn out onto a wire tray to cool. Decorate with cherries and angelica.

INGREDIENTS

Metric		Imperial
30ml	Golden syrup	1oz
28g	Light brown soft sugar	1oz
340g	Can of pineapple rings	12oz
	3 eggs, size 2	
85g	Caster sugar	3oz
85g	Plain flour	3oz

DECORATION

Glacé cherries, cut in half
Angelica, cut into diamonds

BAKING TIN

21.5cm (8½in) round sponge tin greased with butter, base lined with greaseproof paper and greased with more butter.

BAKING

Preheated oven, 180°C or 360°F or gas mark 4
Middle shelf
40-45 minutes.

1. *Sift together the flour, cocoa powder and baking powder. Whisk the egg yolks and sugar together until stiff.*

INGREDIENTS

Metric		Imperial
90g	Plain flour	3¼oz
21g	Cocoa powder	¾oz
3ml	Baking powder	½ heaped tsp
	5 eggs, size 2 separated	
145g	Caster sugar	5oz
115g	Ground walnuts	4oz
40ml	Hot water	4dsp

TOPPING

85g	Caster sugar	3oz
300ml	Double cream	½pt
	Walnuts	
	Chocolate pieces	

BAKING TIN

33 x 23cm (13 x 9in) swiss roll tin, greased and lined with greaseproof paper, then greased.

BAKING

Preheated oven, 180°C or 360°F or gas mark 4
Middle shelf
20 minutes

Mary's Tips

This makes a denser, richer swiss roll than the ordinary fatless one, and therefore makes a perfect dinner party pudding.

Ensure you chill the cream before whisking. A hand (balloon & spiral) whisk gives good results but involves hard work. Avoid using a large electric beater as it is easy to overwhip the cream. Remember to use a big bowl to provide plenty of space for introducing air into the cream.

Whipped cream freezes well by itself in a rigid covered container for up to 4 months. However, once the whipped cream is applied to the cake it should be consumed that day.

2. *Fold in the ground walnuts. Whisk the egg whites until stiff then fold in. Add the hot water and fold in.*

3. *Fold in the sieved ingredients. Spread evenly into the tin and bake. Lay a piece of greaseproof paper on a damp tea-towel and sprinkle with caster sugar.*

4. *When baked turn out onto the paper and immediately roll up. Leave on a wire tray until cold.*

5. *Whisk the cream until firm. Unroll the sponge and spread most of the cream on top.*

WALNUT ROLL

Serves 10-12

6. *Sprinkle chopped walnuts over the cream.*

7. *Gently roll up the sponge and sprinkle top with caster sugar if required. Place onto the serving dish or plate.*

8. *Pipe remaining cream on top and decorate with walnuts and pieces of chocolate.*

BATTENBURG
Serves 8-12

HOWARD RUBY

INGREDIENTS

Metric		Imperial
225g	Butter or margarine	8oz
225g	Caster sugar	8oz
	4 eggs, size 3, lightly beaten	
225g	Plain flour, sifted	8oz
5ml	Baking powder	1tsp
	Pink food colouring	
	Almond essence	
	Vanilla essence	

FILLING

Raspberry seedless jam

COVERING

225g	Marzipan	8oz
	Caster sugar for rolling	
	Apricot puree	
	Cherries	
	Angelica	

BAKING TINS

Two 905g (2lb) loaf tins greased and base lined.

BAKING

Preheated oven, 180°C or 360°F or gas mark 4
Middle shelf
40-45 minutes

Mary's Tips

Go gently with the colouring for this recipe. The pink can be a very light shade to achieve the desired effect. Bakers often use a hard pink in the shops to attract the eye but it is not necessary in the home produced cake.

1. Beat the butter and sugar together until light and fluffy. Then thoroughly beat in the egg, a little at a time.

2. Sift the flour and baking powder together and blend into the batter, using a spoon, until clear.

3. Divide the mixture by weight, in half into separate bowls. Mix pink colour and almond essence in one, then vanilla into the other. Place into tins and bake.

4. When baked turn out onto a wire tray to cool. Then trim the sides, cut into strips and layer with the jam filling.

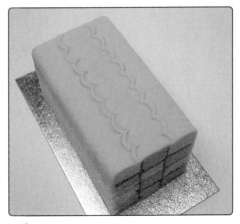

5. Roll out the marzipan, using caster sugar as dusting. Warm apricot puree, brush onto marzipan and wrap around cake. Crimp a pattern on the top.

6. Decorate with cherries and angelica diamonds.

WINE FRUIT CAKE

Serves 16-20

JACOBEAN FLORAL

Mary's Tips

This cake can be wrapped in waxed paper and stored in a cupboard for up to 3 months.

Very good quality cake which can be eaten on its own or used for special occasions such as a wedding.

INGREDIENTS

Metric		Imperial
170g	Block margarine	6oz
120ml	Golden syrup	8 level tbsp
285g	Seedless raisins	10oz
225g	Currants	8oz
145g	Sultanas	5oz
145g	Cut mixed peel	5oz
85g	Glacé cherries, cut into quarters	3oz
200ml	Red table wine	7oz
	3 eggs, size 2	
285g	Plain flour	10oz

1 rounded tsp mixed spice, 1 level tsp nutmeg
Pinch of salt, ½tsp bicarbonate of soda

BAKING TIN

20.5cm (8in) round or 18cm (7in) square deep tin greased with white fat, then lined with greaseproof paper then the paper greased.

BAKING

Preheated oven, 140°C or 285°F or gas mark 1
Centre of oven
1¼-2 hours

1. Place margarine, syrup, fruit and wine into a saucepan over gentle heat. Stir until margarine has melted. Bring to boil and gently cook for 5 minutes.

2. Pour the mixture into a bowl. When cold beat in the eggs. Sift together the flour, spice, nutmeg, salt and bicarbonate of soda into a mixing bowl.

3. Add fruit mixture to flour and mix well. Place in tin, level the top and bake. When baked leave in tin for 30 minutes before turning out onto a wire tray.

MIXED FRUIT TEABREAD

Serves 8

FORGET-ME-NOT

Mary's Tips

Double the recipe and divide between four 445g (1lb) loaf tins.

Freezes well.

This is a very moist teabread and can be eaten without butter. Best eaten 1-2 days after baking.

INGREDIENTS

Metric		Imperial
170g	Raisins	6oz
115g	Sultanas	4oz
57g	Currants	2oz
115g	Light brown soft sugar	4oz
300ml	Cold tea	½pt
	1 egg, size 2, beaten	
45ml	Golden syrup	3tbsp
225g	Plain wholemeal flour	8oz
7.5ml	Baking powder	1½ level tsp
2.5ml	Mixed spice	½ level tsp

BAKING TIN

905g (2lb) loaf tin greased and base lined.

BAKING

Preheated oven, 170°C or 340°F or gas mark 3
Middle shelf
40-60 minutes

1. Soak the fruit and sugar in the cold tea for 12 hours.

2. Beat in the egg and the syrup. Sift the flour, baking powder and mixed spice together.

3. Fold into the mixture and mix well. Spoon into the tins and loosely cover with foil. Bake in preheated oven. Cool on a wire tray. Wrap in foil when cold.

SOUR CREAM and NUT CAKE

Serves 10

1. Cream the butter and sugar until light and fluffy. Thoroughly beat in the egg a little at a time. Then beat in the sour cream.

2. Sift together the flour, salt, baking powder and soda, then beat into the creamed mixture to form a smooth batter.

INGREDIENTS

Metric		Imperial
90g	Butter	3¼oz
80g	Caster sugar	2¾oz
	1 egg, size 3, lightly beaten	
7ml	Sour cream	2½oz
145g	Plain flour	5oz
	Pinch of salt	
5ml	Baking powder	1tsp
1.25ml	Baking soda	¼tsp
	Vanilla flavour	

FILLING AND TOPPING

50g	Caster sugar	1¾oz
2.5ml	Cinnamon	½tsp
30g	Toasted almonds	1oz

BAKING TIN

21.5cm (8½in) brioche tin, well greased.

BAKING

Preheated oven, 160°C or 320°F or gas mark 2½
Middle shelf
45-50 minutes

Mary's Tips

Make sure you leave enough topping for the final layer of the cake. If it looks short, scatter on a few extra flaked almonds, toasted.

When breaking eggs, I recommend the use of a teaspoon to remove any pieces of shell which could fall into the bowl. Try not to store eggs in the fridge in the trays. Eggs keep much better in their covered cartons.

3. Mix all the filling and topping ingredients together in a separate bowl.

4. Place a ⅓rd of the batter into the tin, then sprinkle on a ⅓rd of the filling.

5. Spread ½ the remaining batter on top, then filling, then repeat again with remainders. After baking leave in tin until cold.

VINE HARVEST

LEMON BANANA CAKE

Serves 10-12

1. Cream the butter until light and fluffy. Thoroughly beat in the sugar. Add the essence, beaten eggs and mashed bananas and mix well.

2. Sift together the flour, bicarbonate of soda and salt then blend into the mixture, using a spoon.

3. Spread the mixture into the two tins evenly, using a palette knife. After baking leave in the tins for 5 minutes then turn out onto a wire tray until cold.

INGREDIENTS

Metric		Imperial
255g	Plain flour	9oz
2.5ml	Bicarbonate of soda	½tsp
	Pinch of salt	
115g	Butter or margarine	4oz
170g	Caster sugar	6oz
	A few drops of lemon essence	
	2 eggs, size 3, beaten	
	2 medium bananas, mashed	
150ml	Sour milk	¼pt

FILLING

57g	Butter	2oz
85g	Icing sugar	3oz
	Lemon curd	

TOPPING

15ml	Lemon juice	1tbsp
145g	Icing sugar	5oz
	Dried fruits	

BAKING TINS

Two 18.5cm (7¼in) round sandwich tins greased and base lined.

BAKING

Preheated oven, 190°C or 370°F or gas mark 5
Middle shelf
30 minutes

Mary's Tips

Ripe brown bananas are much better for cakes than unblemished yellow ones. Mash them with a fork or purée them in a blender or food processor.

Although this recipe can make use of ripe bananas. Be careful not to use old lemons for the juice. A very small amount can produce a wooden taste to the cake.

The lemon glacé icing provides an excellent sweet-sour taste to round off the cake. However, this icing will not retain its glossiness for long. I occasionally mix in some stock syrup to make it smooth and glossy.

4. *For the filling, beat the butter and icing sugar until light and fluffy. Spread over one sponge then pipe the lemon curd and place other sponge on top.*

5. *For the topping, pour the lemon juice into a saucepan and stir in the icing sugar. Stir over heat until the icing is just warm to the touch.*

6. *Quickly spread the icing on top then decorate with the fruits.*

SPICY PLUM AND SYRUP CAKE

Serves 16

INGREDIENTS

Metric		Imperial
445g	Self raising flour	1lb
	Pinch of salt	
5ml	Allspice	1tsp
225g	Margarine	8oz
115g	Soft light brown sugar	4oz
225g	Hard margarine	8oz
115g	Raisins	4oz
445g	Fresh plums	1lb
120ml	Golden syrup	8tbsp
	4 eggs, size 3	

TOPPING

45ml	Soft light brown sugar	3tbsp
5ml	Allspice	1tsp

BAKING TIN

21.5cm (8½in) round cake tin greased and fully lined.

BAKING

Preheated oven, 180°C or 360°F or gas mark 4
Middle shelf
1¼ hours

Wrap the cake in foil and keep for at least two days before eating.

1. Sift the flour, salt and spice into a mixing bowl. Cut margarine into pieces then rub into the flour to form a fine crumbly mix. Stir in sugar and raisins.

2. Cut plums in half, remove stones. Put 10-12 halves aside, chop remaining into small pieces. Beat the syrup and eggs together then blend into mixture with plums.

3. Spoon mixture into the tin and level. Place plum halves on top. Mix topping ingredients together and sprinkle on top then bake. Leave in the tin until cold.

PARADISE CAKE

Serves 16-20

INGREDIENTS

Metric		Imperial
285g	Block margarine	10oz
285g	Light brown soft sugar	10oz
	5 eggs, size 2	
1.25ml	Almond essence	¼tsp
315g	Plain flour	11oz
2.5ml	Baking powder	½tsp
42g	Ground almonds	1½oz
145g	Glacé cherries, chopped	5oz
57g	Angelica, chopped	2oz
170g	Crystallised fruits, chopped	6oz

DECORATION

Wide selection of crystallised fruits as required.
Clear jelly.

BAKING

Preheated oven, 150°C or 300°F or gas mark 2
Middle shelf
Approximately 2½ hours

BAKING TIN

21.5cm (8½in) brioche tin, well greased.

1. Beat the margarine and sugar until light. Beat in the egg, a little at a time. Add the essence. Sift the flour and baking powder then fold into the mixture.

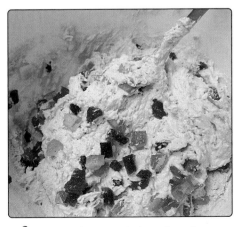

2. Fold in the ground almonds and chopped fruits. Mix until well blended. Place into tin. Bake, leave for 15 mins, then upturn onto a wire tray until cold.

3. When cold glaze the top with jelly, place crystallised fruits on top then cover with more jelly. Leave until set.

COFFEE SULTANA CAKE

Serves 16-20

INGREDIENTS

Metric		Imperial
145g	Butter or margarine	5oz
145g	Light brown soft sugar	5oz
	2 eggs, size 3	
20ml	Coffee extract	2½tsp
225g	Plain flour	8oz
2.5ml	Baking powder	½tsp
115g	Sultanas	4oz
	Milk to mix	

TOPPING

Mixed chopped nuts
Pecan nuts

BAKING TIN

905g (2lb) loaf tin greased and base lined.

BAKING

Preheated oven, 190°C or 370°F or gas mark 5
Middle shelf
1-1¼ hours

1. Cream the butter and sugar and thoroughly beat in the eggs a little at a time. Beat in the coffee extract.

2. Sift together the flour and baking powder. Stir into the mixture with the sultanas and sufficient milk to make a soft consistency.

3. Place mixture into the tin. Sprinkle with chopped nuts then place pecan nuts on top. After baking leave for 10 minutes then turn out onto a wire tray to cool.

HURRELL LOAF

Serves 16

CHINESE GARDEN

INGREDIENTS

Metric		Imperial
170g	Wholemeal flour	6oz
	Self raising flour	
115g	Baking powder	4oz
2.5ml	Pinch of nutmeg	½ tsp
170g	Sultanas	6oz
57g	Walnuts, chopped	2oz
115g	Demerara sugar	4oz
225ml	Black treacle	8oz
200ml	Milk	¼pt plus 3tbsp

BAKING TIN

905g (2lb) loaf tin, lightly greased and base lined.

BAKING

Preheated oven, 170°C or 340°F or gas mark 3
Middle shelf
1-1¼ hours

1. Put the wholemeal flour into a bowl, sift in the plain flour together with the baking powder and nutmeg. Stir in the sultanas, walnuts and sugar.

2. Pour the treacle into a saucepan, add the milk and stir over low heat until the liquids combine. Pour the liquid into the dry ingredients and mix well.

3. Spoon the mixture into the tin and bake. After baking leave in the tin for 15 minutes then turn out onto a wire tray to cool. Serve sliced and buttered.

1. *Sieve the flour, cornflour and baking powder into a mixing bowl. Rub in the margarine and stir in the sugar and sultanas.*

2. *Mix to a soft dough with the beaten egg and milk.*

Metric		Imperial
170g	Plain flour	6oz
57g	Cornflour	2oz
10ml	Baking powder	2tsp
115g	Light brown sugar	4oz
115g	Margarine	4oz
57g	Sultanas	2oz
	1 egg, size 3	
90ml	Milk	6tbsp

TOPPING

57g	Plain flour	2oz
57g	Demerara sugar	2oz
15ml	Cinnamon	1tbsp
28g	Margarine	1oz

BAKING TIN

21.5cm (8½in) sponge tin, greased.

BAKING

Preheated oven at 190°C or 375°F or gas mark 5, for 45 minutes.

Mary's Tips

This cake is most delicious when eaten while still warm.

Demerara sugar has about 2 per cent molasses in it. Dark brown Muscovado sugar has about 13 per cent molasses. Be wary of using Muscovado sugar on delicate cakes as the molasses will darken the colour and can alter the flavour. Its soft, fine texture make it ideal for fruit cakes.

3. *Put the mixture into a greased sponge tin, and smooth over with a spatula.*

4. *Make the topping by rubbing the margarine into the flour, sugar and cinnamon.*

5. *Spoon this over the raw cake mixture and bake for about 45 minutes.*

CINNAMON CRUMBLE CAKE

Serves 10

WARMSTRY WHITE

APPLE GINGERBREAD RING

Serves 12-16

INGREDIENTS A

Metric		Imperial
225g	Plain flour	8oz
2.5ml	Salt	½tsp
7.5ml	Ground ginger	1½tsp
7.5ml	Baking powder	1½tsp
2.5ml	Bicarbonate of soda	½tsp

Step 1. Sift the ingredients listed in A together into a large bowl.

INGREDIENTS B

Metric		Imperial
115g	Light brown soft sugar	4oz
85g	Butter or margarine	3oz
28ml	Black treacle	1oz
115ml	Golden syrup	4oz

Step 2. Place all the ingredients listed in B into a saucepan and gently heat until the butter melts.

INGREDIENTS C

Metric		Imperial
150ml	Milk	¼pt
	1 egg, size 2	

Step 3. Pour the milk into a separate saucepan and warm slightly, remove from the heat, and beat in the egg.

GLAZE

57ml (2oz) golden syrup
150ml (¼pt) water
2.5ml (½tsp) ground ginger
10ml (2tsp) arrowroot
30ml (2tbsp) preserved stem ginger syrup

For the glaze, pour the syrup and water into a saucepan, bring to the boil and simmer for 5 minutes. Blend together the ground ginger, arrowroot and ginger syrup in a separate bowl. Pour on the hot syrup, stir well and return to the pan. Continue boiling and stirring for 2 minutes.

FILLING

3 eating apples, cored, peeled, sliced and washed in lemon juice to stop browning
16 whole stoned dates
2 large pieces of preserved stem ginger, cut into thin strips.

BAKING TIN

20.5cm (8in) ring mould well greased.

BAKING

Preheated oven, 180°C or 360°F or gas mark 4
Middle shelf
35 minutes approximately

1. Follow steps one to three in the ingredients listing then blend liquid mixtures into the dry ingredients, using a spoon.

2. Pour the mixture into the prepared tin and immediately place into the oven and bake.

3. When baked leave in the tin for 5 minutes then upturn onto a wire tray to cool.

Mary's Tips

Plain flour is essential for this recipe. The raising agent in self raising flour would conflict with the bicarbonate of soda, which is necessary for the dark gingerbread colour.

I strongly recommend the mixture of Golden syrup and black treacle in B. Black treacle alone gives a bitter taste and golden syrup alone, an anaemic cake. If the cooked cake is doughy or sunk in the middle, you have probably used too much syrup.

MOUNTBATTEN BLUE

4. Follow the instructions for making the glaze.

5. Add the prepared sliced apples to the glaze and poach for 10-15 minutes, or until just tender.

6. Strain the apples and place into the centre of the cake with the dates and ginger. Then brush the glaze over the cake.

65

APPLE, DATE and COCONUT CAKE

Serves 8-10

Mary's Tips

It is best to use a dessert apple for this cake, rather than a cooker. I used Golden Delicious, but any variety will do. The cake can also be glazed with melted apricot jam if required. It is best eaten fresh, but does freeze well too.

INGREDIENTS

Metric		Imperial
285g	Self raising flour	10oz
57g	Desiccated coconut	2oz
85g	Dates, chopped	3oz
85g	Block margarine	3oz
42g	Trex	1½oz
130g	Caster sugar	4½oz
	1 medium sized apple	
	3 eggs, size 2	

BAKING TIN

16.5cm (6½in) round cake tin greased and fully lined with greaseproof paper.

BAKING

Preheated oven, 180°C or 360°F or gas mark 4
Middle shelf
1¼ hours

1. Sift the flour into a bowl then stir in the coconut. Add the chopped dates. Rub in the margarine and Trex until mixture resembles fine breadcrumbs.

2. Stir in sugar. Peel and core apple then chop half into small squares and add to mixture. Beat the eggs and stir into mixture to blend ingredients evenly.

3. When cold glaze the top with jelly, place crystallised fruits on top then cover with more jelly. Leave until set.

ROSE MARBLED CAKE

Serves 14-16

VICEROY SILVER

INGREDIENTS

Metric		Imperial	Metric		
170g	Butter	6oz	57g	Ground almonds	2oz
170g	Caster sugar	6oz		A little milk if necessary	
2.5ml	Almond essence	½tsp			
	3 eggs, size 3, lightly beaten			Food colouring of choice	
225g	Self raising flour sifted with a pinch of salt	8oz	15ml	Cocoa powder	1tbsp

BAKING TIN

16.5cm (6½in) round cake tin greased and lined.

BAKING

Preheated oven, 180°C or 360°F or gas mark 4
Middle shelf
50-60 minutes

1. Cream butter and sugar until light and fluffy, add essence. Beat in the eggs a little at a time. Fold in the flour and ground almonds, add milk if too stiff.

2. Divide the mixture into three equal parts. Leave one plain, colour the second with pink food colouring and add the cocoa powder to the third.

3. Place alternate spoonfuls into the tin, keeping colours evenly dispersed. After baking leave in the tin for 20 minutes then place onto a wire tray until cold.

67

RICH CHOCOLATE CAKE

Serves 16-20

BOURNEMOUTH

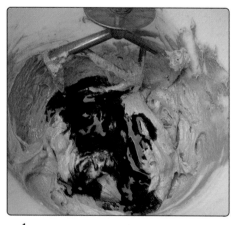

1. CAKE. *Beat together the butter and sugar. Thoroughly beat in the egg a little at a time. Stir in the treacle and essence.*

2. Sift together the flour, bicarbonate of soda, baking powder and salt. Fold into the creamed mixture.

3. Gradually fold in melted chocolate and sufficient milk to make into a thick batter. Divide mixture between tins and bake. Turn out onto a wire tray to cool.

4. FUDGE ICING. *Place all the ingredients into a heavy-based saucepan and heat gently, stirring until the sugar has melted.*

5. *Bring to the boil and cook to 116°C (240°F) or until the syrup, when dropped into cold water, will form a soft ball which can be squashed.*

INGREDIENTS

Metric		Imperial
145g	Butter	5oz
285g	Dark brown soft sugar	10oz
	3 eggs, size 3	
30ml	Black treacle	1oz
5ml	Vanilla essence	1tsp
225g	Plain flour	8oz
2.5ml	Bicarbonate of soda	½tsp
10ml	Baking powder	2tsp
	Pinch of salt	
225ml	Milk	8oz
57g	Cooking or plain chocolate, melted	2oz

FILLING

170g	Chocolate buttercream (see p5)	6oz

FUDGE ICING

455g	Caster sugar	1lb
150ml	Milk	¼pt
115g	Butter	4oz
30ml	Golden syrup	1oz
15ml	Cocoa powder	1tsp
57g	Cooking or plain chocolate	2oz

DECORATION

Chocolate curls
Cocoa powder

BAKING TIN

Two 21.5cm (8½in) round sandwich tin, greased.

BAKING

Preheated oven, 180°C or 360°F or gas mark 4
Middle shelf
30-35 minutes

Mary's Tips

Surprisingly little heat is required to soften chocolate. I recommend breaking the chocolate in a bowl over a saucepan of hot water, away from the heat source. Leave until melted. The smaller the chocolate blocks the easier (and faster) the process. Ensure no moisture enters the bowl. If you have a microwave, chocolate can easily be melted in it. Keep a close eye on progress to check the chocolate is not separated or even burnt.

6. *Remove from heat and leave to cool for 10 minutes, then beat until it is thick enough to spread.*

7. *Sandwich the sponges together with buttercream filling. Then quickly spread the fudge over the top and sides. Leave until set.*

8. *Decorate the cake-top with chocolate curls and then dust with cocoa powder.*

APPLE and WALNUT TEABREAD

Serves 8-10

1. Sift together the flour, salt and mixed spice into a large bowl. Add all of the remaining ingredients.

2. Beat well together, using a spoon, to form an even blended mixture. Place mixture into the tin and level.

3. Sprinkle the top with a good layer of demerara sugar. After baking leave in the tin for 10 minutes then turn out onto a wire tray to cool.

ARCADIA

INGREDIENTS

Metric		Imperial
225g	Self raising flour	8oz
	Pinch of salt	
5ml	Mixed spice	1tsp
115g	Soft tub margarine	4oz
115g	Caster sugar	4oz
	2 egg, size 2	
15ml	Golden syrup	1tsp
115g	Sultanas	4oz
57g	Walnuts, chopped	2oz
	1 medium cooking apple, peeled, cored and chopped.	

BAKING TIN

905g (2lb) loaf tin greased and base lined.

BAKING

Preheated oven, 180°C or 360°F or gas mark 4 for 1 hour then reduce heat to 170°C or 340°F or gas mark 3 for 20 minutes or until baked.

Mary's Tips

Teabread is often served with butter, but this one is so moist already that it is an unnecessary addition.

70

ORIENTAL CAKE

Serves 8-12

VINE HARVEST

EVESHAM GOLD

INGREDIENTS

Metric		Imperial
340g	Plain flour	12oz
	Pinch of salt	
170g	Butter or margarine	6oz
225g	Caster sugar	8oz
215ml	Milk	7½oz
	4 egg whites, size 2, beaten	
5ml	Cinnamon	1tsp
5ml	Grated nutmeg	1tsp
170g	Figs, finely chopped	6oz
15ml	Golden syrup, warmed	1tbsp

BAKING TIN

21.5cm (8½in) round cake tin greased and fully lined with greaseproof paper.

BAKING

Preheated oven, 175°C or 350°F or gas mark 3½
Middle shelf
35-40 minutes

1. Sift the flour and salt together. Cream the butter and sugar, add the flour and the milk then fold in the beaten egg whites.

2. Divide the mixture in half; leave one half plain, and to the other add the spices, figs and syrup.

3. Place alternate spoonfuls of the two mixtures into the tin. After baking leave for 15 minutes then turn out onto a wire tray and dust with caster sugar.

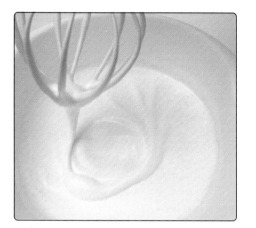

1. *Melt the butter in a saucepan over gentle heat. Then remove from the heat. Whisk the eggs and sugar in a bowl over hot water until light and fluffy.*

2. *Remove the water and whisk until the mixture is cool. Sift the flours together and fold half into the mixture. Fold in half the melted butter.*

Metric		Imperial	
42g	Butter, melted	1½oz	
	3 eggs, size 2		
85g	Caster sugar	3oz	
71g	Plain flour	2½oz	
15ml	Cornflour	1tbsp	

FILLING

	Raspberry seedless jam		
285ml	Double cream, whipped	10oz	
	Icing sugar for dusting		
	1 glacé cherry		

Two sponges are required, therefore double the mixture if your own is large enough to take both tins for baking. If not make and bake one at a time.

BAKING TIN

21.5cm (8¼in) round sandwich tin greased and base lined.

BAKING

Preheated oven, 180°C or 360°F or gas mark 4
Middle shelf
25-30 minutes

Mary's Tips

To make a light sponge, slightly warm the flour. If you allow the flour to be cold, it will chill the eggs which will release some of the air just beaten in. Remember, air is the only rising agent in a Genoese and you should do everything possible to incorporate and retain as much as possible.

Do not attempt to use granulated sugar as a substitute for caster sugar. It dissolves less easily and gives a speckly surface.

When cutting cold Genoese, I suggest twisting the knife from left to right. You may find a straight cut produces a ragged and crumbly edge.

3. *Gradually fold in remaining butter and flour alternately. Pour into tin and bake. After baking turn out onto a wire tray to cool. Cut out centre of one sponge.*

4. *Spread jam over the base sponge, place the ring on top. Fill the centre with the whipped cream to form a peak.*

5. *Cut the circle into required sections and place onto the cream. Then dust lightly with sifted icing sugar. Decorate with a glacé cherry.*

GENOESE SPONGE CAKE

Serves 16

HOWARD LEATHER GREEN

SYRUP TEABREAD

Serves 12

FRANCESCA

INGREDIENTS

Metric		Imperial
170g	Self raising flour	**6oz**
5ml	Ground ginger	**1tsp**
	Pinch of salt	
45ml	Vegetable oil	**3tbsp**
60ml	Golden syrup	**4tbsp**
57g	Demerara sugar	**2oz**
	1 egg, size 3	
30ml	Milk	**2tbsp**
85g	Sultanas	**3oz**

TOPPING

15ml (1tbsp) golden syrup, warmed
15g (½oz) glacé cherries, chopped
15g (½oz) walnuts, chopped

BAKING TIN

455g (1lb) loaf tin greased and base lined.

BAKING

Preheated oven, 180°C or 360°F or gas mark 4
Middle shelf
1 hour
Cover the cake with foil if it becomes too dark during baking.

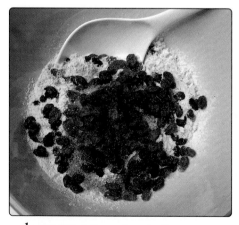

1. CAKE. *Sift together the flour, cinnamon and salt into a large bowl. Add all the remaining ingredients.*

2. Stir the ingredients together then beat for 2-3 minutes until well blended. Pour the mixture into the tin and bake.

3. When baked leave in tin for 5 mins. then turn out onto a wire tray to cool. TOPPING. *Brush top with syrup, sprinkle with chopped cherries and walnuts.*

APRICOT NUT BREAD

Serves 12-16

INGREDIENTS

Metric		Imperial
340g	Self raising flour	12oz
	Pinch of salt	
115g	Caster sugar	4oz
145g	Chopped dried apricots	5oz
57g	Blanched almonds, chopped	2oz
	Grated rind of 1 lemon	
	4 eggs, size 3	
150ml	Sour cream	5oz
57g	Melted butter	2oz
	Milk if required	

TOPPING

115g (4oz) icing sugar
Juice of 1 lemon

To make the topping, sift the icing sugar into a bowl and beat in sufficient lemon juice to make a thickish soft icing.

DECORATION

A few apricots, chopped

BAKING TIN

905g (2lb) loaf tin greased and base lined.

BAKING

Preheated oven, 170°C or 340°F or gas mark 3
Middle shelf
1½ hours approximately

1. Sift together the flour and salt into a bowl. Stir in the sugar, apricots, almonds and grated lemon rind. Make a well in the centre.

2. Whisk together the eggs, cream and melted butter then stir into the mixture to make a soft, dropping consistency adding a little milk if necessary.

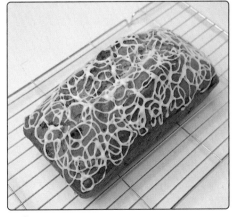

3. Place mixture evenly into the tin and bake. After baking leave for 10 minutes then turn out onto a wire tray to cool. Decorate with topping.

RUM and CARAMEL LAYER

Serves 16-20

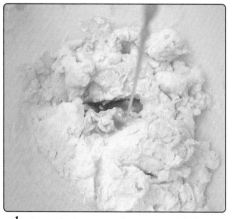

1. Beat the butter and sugar until light and fluffy. Gradually beat in the egg yolks. Sift dry ingredients together, fold in with alternate spoonfuls of the liquids.

2. Beat egg whites until stiff, gently fold into mixture. Divide mixture between the tins and bake. After baking, cool for 5 minutes then turn out onto a wire tray.

3. Beat all filling ingredients together until fluffy. Slice and sandwich the cakes together. Leave some filling for the sides. Brush top with boiling apricot purée.

4. Place all ingredients for the toffee (except the vinegar) into a saucepan and heat gently. When boiling add the vinegar, stirring occasionally.

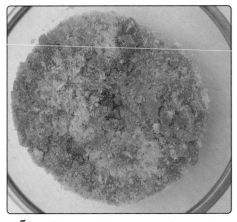

5. Boil for 10-15 minutes until caramel in colour. Then pour out onto a greased, non-stick tray and spread thinly. When cold break into small pieces.

INGREDIENTS

Metric		Imperial
145g	Butter or margarine, softened	5oz
115g	Caster sugar	4oz
	2 eggs, size 2, separated	
225g	Plain flour	8oz
	Pinch of salt	
10ml	Baking powder	2tsp
115g	Orange juice	4oz
115ml	Rum	4oz

RUM CREAM FILLING

115g	Butter	4oz
340g	icing sugar, sifted	12oz
	2 egg whites, size 3, stiffly beaten	
	Rum flavouring	

TOFFEE FOR CAKE SIDES

225g	Caster sugar	8oz
28g	Butter	1oz
5ml	Golden syrup	1tsp
75ml	Water	⅛ pint
2.5ml	Vinegar	½tsp

GLACÉ ICING

225g	Icing sugar, sifted	8oz
	Few drops of flavouring	
	Approximately 45ml (3tbsp) water	
	Food colourings	

BAKING TINS

Two 18.5cm (7¼in) square tins greased and fully lined.

BAKING

Preheated oven, 180°C or 360°F or gas mark 4
Middle shelf
25 minutes

Mary's Tips

Though this recipe asks for rum flavouring in the cream filling, the real thing can certainly be used.

6. For the glacé icing, mix ingredients together, adjust water so that the consistency coats the back of a spoon. Colour a small amount for the lines.

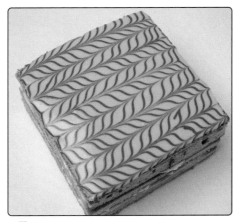

7. Fill a piping bag with dark icing. Coat cake-top with main icing, then pipe lines one way and draw a cocktail stick across the other to form feathering.

8. When the icing has set, spread the sides with cream then cover with the toffee pieces.

INGREDIENTS
(for Rich Jamaican Loaf)

Metric		Imperial
85g	Margarine	3oz
115g	Light brown sugar	4oz
15ml	Golden syrup	1tbsp
15ml	Black treacle	1tbsp
	2 eggs, size 3, beaten	
225g	Mashed banana	8oz
225g	Self-raising flour	8oz
5ml	Mixed spice	1tsp
1.25ml	Bicarbonate of soda	¼tsp
1.25ml	Salt	¼tsp
225g	Raisins	8oz

FOR THE GLAZE

30ml	Warmed golden syrup	2tbsp

BAKING TIN

21.5 x 11.5cm (8½ x 4½in) loaf tin, greased and lined.

BAKING

Preheated oven at 180°C or 30°F or gas mark 4 for about 1½ hours.

INGREDIENTS
(for Yoghurt Loaf)

Metric		Imperial
115g	Plain flour	4oz
5ml	Baking powder	1tsp
2.5ml	Bicarbonate of soda	½tsp
2.5ml	Mixed spice	½tsp
2.5ml	Nutmeg	½tsp
2.5ml	Star aniseed	½tsp
115g	Wholemeal flour	4oz
170g	Light brown sugar	6oz
	2 eggs, size 2	
75g	Sunflower oil	3oz
145g	Carton of black cherry yoghurt	6oz

BAKING TIN

21.5 x 11.5cm (8½ x 4½in) loaf tin, greased and lined.

BAKING

Preheated oven at 180°C or 30°F or gas mark 4 for about 1 hour.

RICH JAMAICAN LOAF

1. Cream the margarine and sugar together until light and fluffy. Stir in the treacle and syrup. Add the eggs and banana, and mix well.

2. Sieve the flour, spice, bicarbonate of soda and salt, and add to the creamed mixture with the raisins. Place in the greased and lined loaf tin.

3. Bake until well-risen and firm to the touch: about 1½ hours. Remove from tin, then glaze the top with melted golden syrup.

RICH JAMAICAN LOAF and YOGHURT LOAF
Each Serves 10

MARQUIS

YOGHURT LOAF

1. Sieve the plain flour, baking powder, bicarbonate of soda and spices. Add the wholemeal flour and the sugar.

2. Beat the eggs and add to the dry mixture with the oil and the yoghurt. Stir until smooth. Put into the prepared tin.

3. Bake for about 1 hour or until well-risen and golden in colour. Test with a skewer, it should come out clean. Cool on a wire tray.

BUTTER MADEIRA CAKE

Serves 10

Mary's Tips

Though this cake was traditionally eaten in the 19th century with a glass of Madeira wine in the morning, it is now widely regarded as a classic teatime cake.

INGREDIENTS

Metric		Imperial
170g	Butter	6oz
170g	Caster sugar	6oz
	3 eggs, size 3, beaten	
145g	Self-raising flour	5oz
115g	Plain flour	4oz
	Grated rind and juice of one orange	
28g	Crushed cube sugar	1oz
	Few strands of crystallised orange peel	

BAKING TIN

905g (2lb) loaf tin, greased

BAKING

Preheated oven at 170°C or 325°F or gas mark 3 for about 1 hour 15 minutes.

1. Beat together the butter and sugar until light. Beat in the eggs, one at a time. Fold in the flours.

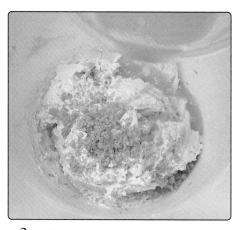

2. Add the rind and juice of an orange, and stir well.

3. Put into the prepared tin, and smooth over. Sprinkle the crushed sugar and a few strands of crystallised orange peel over the top.

SULTANA and APPLE SCONE

Serves 8

1. Peel, core and finely chop the apple. Sift together flour, salt and baking powder. Rub in butter, then add sugar, apple and sultanas.

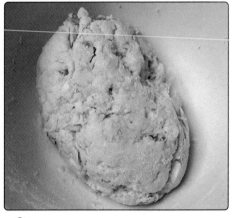

2. Mix to a soft, but not sticky dough with the beaten egg and a little milk.

3. Roll out on a floured table to 0.5cm (¼in) thick and about 20cm (8in) diameter. Make into 8 wedges and brush with a little milk and sugar before baking.

INGREDIENTS

Metric		Imperial
	1 medium cooking apple	
57g	Sultanas	2oz
225g	Self-raising flour, sifted	8oz
2.5ml	Salt	½tsp
5ml	Baking powder	1tsp
57g	Butter	2oz
57g	Caster sugar	2oz
	1 egg, size 3	
	Enough milk to mix to a soft dough	

FOR THE GLAZE

A little milk and caster sugar

BAKING TIN

21.5cm (8½in) round sandwich or flan tin.

BAKING

Preheted oven at 200°C or 400°F or gas mark 6 for about 20 minutes.

Mary's Tips

Serve wedges of the scone while still warm, spread with butter.

QUICKIE SPONGE CAKES

1. Melt together the margarine, syrup and sugar over a gentle heat and then leave to cool a little.

2. Beat the egg into the milk and stir into the syrup mixture.

3. Sift flour into a bowl and beat in syrup mixture using a spoon, until smooth. Place into tin and bake. After baking turn out onto a wire tray until cold.

INGREDIENTS FOR BASIC MIXTURE

Metric		Imperial
57g	Margarine	2oz
115g	Golden syrup	4oz
57g	Caster sugar	2oz
	1 egg, size 2	
30ml	Milk	2tbsp
115g	Self raising flour	4oz

BAKING TIN

19cm (7½in) round sponge tin greased and base lined.

BAKING

Preheated oven, 190°C or 370°F or gas mark 5
Middle shelf
25 minutes

Mary's Tips

This cake has the appearance of
a sponge, though it is made by the melting method.
See below for when to add different flavour variations.

COFFEE
Add 10ml (2tsp) of instant coffee to the melted margarine and syrup mixture.

COCONUT
Add 50g (2oz) desicccated coconut to the flour after sifting.

CHOCOLATE
From the bowl of sieved flour, remove 15ml (1tbsp) and replace it with 15ml (1tbsp) cocoa powder.

ORANGE
Grate the rind of an orange finely and add to the raw mixture. Use the juice for glacé icing.

LEMON
As with orange, add the grated rind to the mixture, and use the lemon juice for glacé icing to cover the cake.

ALMOND
For a moist, rich cake, add 50g (2oz) of ground almonds to the flour after sifting.

83

GERMAN APPLE CAKE

Serves 10-12

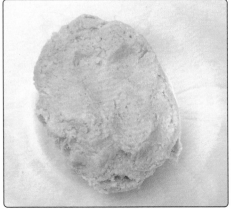

1. BASE. Sift together flour, sugar and half ground almonds. Rub in the butter until mixture resembles fine crumbs. Mix in the egg and juice to form a dough.

2. Press dough evenly into the tin then cover with remaining ground almonds. FILLING. Peel and core apples, cut into slices, mix with sugar and lemon juice.

3. Place the prepared apples over base. TOPPING. Sift together the dry ingredients then mix in butter until crumbly. Sprinkle over apples and bake.

INGREDIENTS

Metric		Imperial
170g	Self raising flour	6oz
85g	Light brown soft sugar	3oz
85g	Ground almonds	3oz
130g	Butter	4½oz
	1 egg, size 3, beaten	
7.5ml	Lemon juice	1½tsp
	FILLING	
680g	Cooking apples	1½tsp
130g	Light brown soft sugar	4½oz
7.5ml	Lemon juice	1½tsp
	TOPPING	
85g	Self raising flour	3oz
215g	Light brown soft sugar	7½oz
7.5ml	Powdered cinnamon	1½tsp
85g	Butter	3oz

BAKING TIN

21.5cm (8½in) round loose-bottomed cake tin greased and base lined.

BAKING

Preheated oven 180°C or 360°F or gas mark 4
Middle shelf
1-1½ hours
When baked leave in the tin until cold before removing. Then dust with icing sugar to serve.

CRUNCHY HAZELNUT CAKE

Serves 16

EVESHAM GOLD AND NAPKIN

INGREDIENTS

Metric		Imperial
130g	Butter or margarine	4½oz
215g	Caster sugar	7½oz
	3 eggs, size 2	
170g	Ground hazelnuts	6oz
515g	Self raising flour, sifted with 1.25ml (¼tsp) salt	18oz
	Milk as required	

DECORATION

57g	Flaked hazelnuts	2oz

Mary's Tips

If flaked hazelnuts are difficult to find, buy whole ones and chop them roughly with a sharp knife on a steady board.

BAKING TIN

23cm (9in) ring tin, well greased.

BAKING

Preheated oven, 190°C or 370°F or gas mark 5 for 30 minutes then reduce heat to 160°C or 320°F or gas mark 2½ until baked.
Middle shelf
Total cooking time 1-1¼ hours

1. Grease the ring tin and place the flaked almonds evenly around the base. Cream the butter, add the sugar and beat until light and fluffy.

2. Beat in the eggs, one at a time. Mix in the ground hazelnuts. Fold in the sifted flour and salt, with sufficient milk to make a fairly soft consistency.

3. Spoon the mixture into the tin and bake. After baking leave in the tin for 30 minutes then turn out onto a wire tray to cool.

SACHERTORTE

Serves 16

SUMMERFIELD

INGREDIENTS

Metric		Imperial
145g	Butter	5oz
145g	Caster sugar	5oz
	5 eggs, size 3, separated	
170g	Plain chocolate, melted	6oz
115g	Plain flour	4oz
28g	Cornflour	1oz
2.5ml	Baking powder	½tsp
1¼ml	Almond essence	¼tsp

FILLING

30ml	Rum	2tbsp
75ml	Seedless raspberry jam	5tbsp

TOPPING

115g	Caster sugar	4oz
145ml	Cold water	5fl.oz
45ml	Warm water	3tbsp
145g	Plain chocolate, melted	5oz

DECORATION

60ml	Milk chocolate melted with a little glycerin to form piping consistency.	2oz

BAKING TIN

21.5cm (8½in) round sandwich tin greased and floured.

BAKING

Preheated oven, 150°C or 300°F or gas mark 2
Middle shelf
45 minutes

Mary's Tips

Sachertorte comes from the tradition of the rich chocolate cake made and served at Sacher's Hotel in Vienna, Austria. It is usually served with cream as a dessert.

1. For the torte, beat the butter and sugar together until light and fluffy. Then thoroughly beat in the egg yolks, one at a time.

2. Gradually add and beat in the melted chocolate, until well blended.

3. Sift the flour, cornflour and baking powder together, then fold into the mixture with a metal spoon.

4. Whisk the egg whites until stiff, fold into the mixture with the essence.

5. Spoon the mixture into the prepared sandwich tin, level then bake for approximately 45 minutes or until baked.

6. After baking leave until cold. For the filling, slice into two or three layers then brush bottom layers with rum and purée. Sandwich together.

7. For the topping, melt the sugar in the cold water over low heat. Do not stir. Boil to 115°C (240°F). Melt the chocolate.

8. When sugar is at 115°C (240°F) immediately remove from heat. Stir the warm water into the chocolate then stir into the boiled sugar.

9. Leave the topping to cool, stirring occasionally to slightly thicken. Pour over the torte and leave to set. Pipe SACHER across the top with milk chocolate.

INGREDIENTS
for Peanut and Orange Teabread

Metric		Imperial
225g	Chunky peanut butter	8oz
57g	Butter or margarine, softened	2oz
285g	Self raising flour	10oz
1.25ml	Salt	¼tsp
115g	Golden syrup	4oz
	2 eggs, size 3	
	Grated rind and juice of 2 oranges	
	Milk	
57g	Salted peanuts	2oz

BAKING TIN

905g (2lb) loaf tin, lightly greased and base lined.

BAKING

Preheated oven, 180°C or 360°F or gas mark 4
Middle shelf
1¼ hours

INGREDIENTS
for Banana Teabread

Metric		Imperial
200g	Self raising flour	7oz
1.25ml	Bicarbonate of soda	¼tsp
2.5ml	Salt	½tsp
85g	Butter or block margarine	3oz
115g	Caster sugar	4oz
	2 eggs, size 3	
225g	Bananas, peeled and mashed	8oz
30ml	Golden syrup	2tbsp
225g	Mixed dried fruit	8oz
115g	Nuts, coarsely chopped	4oz

BAKING TIN

905g (2lb) loaf tin, lightly greased and base lined.

BAKING

Preheated oven, 180°C or 360°F or gas mark 4
Middle shelf
1¼ hours

Wrap in foil and keep for a day before serving sliced and buttered if required.

PEANUT AND ORANGE TEABREAD

1. Place the peanut butter, butter, flour, salt, syrup, eggs and grated rind into a bowl.

2. Make the orange juice up to 225g (8oz) with milk. Add to the mixture and beat with a spoon for about 3 minutes.

3. Place mixture into the tin, sprinkle on the peanuts and bake. After baking turn out onto a wire tray to cool.

FAVOURITE TEABREADS
Each Serves 12

BANANA TEABREAD

1. Sift together the flour, bicarbonate of soda and salt into a bowl. Rub the butter into the flour until the mixture resembles breadcrumbs.

2. Beat the eggs, mashed bananas and syrup together and then stir into the mixture.

3. Stir in the dried fruit and nuts. Place into tin and bake. After baking turn out onto a wire tray to cool.

GLAZED NUT CHRISTMAS CAKE

Serves 30-36

1. *Cream the butter and sugar together. Slowly beat in the eggs. Sift the flour into a separate bowl, then mix in the remaining ingredients (except the beer).*

2. *Stir the dry ingredients into the creamed mixture then add the beer or wine to form a wet consistency. Spoon the mixture into the tin and level.*

3. *Make a decorative pattern using the nuts and cherries, then brush with egg white and bake. Cover the cake top after 2½ hours with greaseproof paper.*

INGREDIENTS

Metric		Imperial
225g	Butter	8oz
225g	Dark brown soft sugar	8oz
285g	Plain flour	10oz
	5 eggs, size 2	
445g	Currants	16oz
340g	Sultanas	12oz
340g	Raisins	12oz
115g	Mixed cut peel	4oz
115g	Glacé cherries, chopped	4oz
57g	Split almonds, chopped	2oz
2.5ml	Mixed spice	½tsp
2.5ml	Nutmeg	½tsp
2.5ml	Cinnamon	½tsp
1.25ml	Ginger	¼tsp
1.25ml	Cloves	¼tsp
	Grated rind of ½ a lemon	
	Grated ring of ¼ an orange	
60ml	Beer or barley wine	4tbsp

TOPPING

Selection of nuts and cherries
Egg white for glazing

BAKING TIN

20.5cm (8in) square cake tin greased and fully lined with greaseproof paper. Tie a piece of thick brown paper round the outside of the tin to protect the cake sides from burning.

BAKING

Preheated oven, 160°C or 320°F or gas mark 2½ for 30 minutes then reduce to 150°C or 300°F or gas mark 2 for 2½ hours and finally to 140°C or 285°F or gas mark 1 for 1 hour.

GINGER CAKE

Serves 16

CHINESE GARDEN

1. Heat the margarine, syrup and sugar in a saucepan until the margarine has fully melted. Do not let the mixture boil. Remove from heat and allow to cool.

2. Sift together flour, salt, ginger and bicarbonate or soda into a bowl. Using a spoon, beat in the warm mixture, the egg, then yoghurt to form a smooth batter.

INGREDIENTS

Metric		Imperial
115g	Margarine	4oz
115ml	Golden syrup	4oz
115g	Dark brown soft sugar	4oz
225g	Plain flour	8oz
	Pinch of salt	
10ml	Ground ginger	2tsp
5ml	Bicarbonate of soda	1tsp
60ml	Plain or blackcherry yoghurt	4tbsp
	1 egg, size 3	

BAKING TIN

18.5cm (7¼in) square sandwich tin greased and fully lined.

BAKING

Preheated oven, 170°C or 340°F or gas mark 3
Lower shelf
55 minutes

Mary's Tips

If eaten straight after baking, it is less necessary to ice this cake. But after a day or two, cover it with fudge frosting, or buttercream or glacé icing, flavoured with 10ml (2tsp) lemon juice, and decorate with pieces of chopped stem ginger, or crystallised ginger.

3. Pour into the tins and bake. When baked leave to cool in the tin. Remove cake from the tin, place on a wire tray.

COUNTRY FARMHOUSE FRUIT CAKE

Serves 20-24

1. Rub the margarine into the sifted flour and baking powder, using fingertips, until mixture resembles breadcrumbs. Stir in the sugar and fruit.

2. Place syrup, eggs and marmalade into a bowl and thoroughly whisk together. Stir into the mixture and mix well.

3. Place into tin and level the top. Sprinkle with demerara sugar and bake. When baked, leave 30 minutes, turn out and leave on wire tray until cold.

INGREDIENTS

Metric		Imperial
255g	Margarine, cut into small pieces	9oz
515g	Plain flour sifted with	18oz
20ml	Baking powder	4tsp
255g	Soft light brown sugar	9oz
255g	Sultanas	9oz
255g	Currants	9oz
45ml	Golden syrup	3tbsp
	5 eggs, size 3	
30ml	Marmalade	2tbsp
	TOPPING	
45ml	Demerara sugar	3tbsp

BAKING

Preheated oven, 150°C or 300°F or gas mark 2
Middle shelf
2½ hours approximately

BAKING TIN

25.5cm (10in) round fluted cake tin, greased and base lined.

Mary's Tips

This extra large farmhouse fruit cake stores well for up to two weeks in a tin, and can also be frozen.

For added flavour soak the fruit overnight in cold tea. You can use up the leftovers at the bottom of your pot.

ORANGE CIDER CAKE

Serves 12

GREEN BAMBOO

INGREDIENTS

Metric		Imperial
115g	Butter or margarine	4oz
170g	Caster sugar	6oz
	2 egg yolks	
225g	Plain flour	8oz
5ml	Baking powder	1tsp
2.5ml	Cinnamon	½tsp
2.5ml	Allspice	½tsp
	Grated rind of 1 orange	
225g	Currants	8oz
150ml	Sweet cider	¼pt

TOPPING

Glacé icing (see p. 77)
Orange flavouring
Coloured coconut

BAKING TIN

15cm (6¼in) round cake tin greased and base lined.

BAKING

Preheated oven, 175°C or 350°F or gas mark 4
Middle shelf
1-1¼ hours

1. Cream together the butter and sugar. Thoroughly beat in the egg yolks, one at a time.

2. Sift together the flour and baking powder, stir in the rind and currants until well mixed.

3. Blend into the creamed butter with the cider. Place into tin and bake. After baking, leave in tin until cold. Cover top with orange flavoured icing and coconut.

STRAWBERRY and ALMOND CAKE

Serves 16

MARQUIS

1. Whisk the eggs and sugar together in a bowl over a pan of hot water, until the mixture is light and thick and holds the shape of a figure 8.

2. Lightly fold in the sieved flour, then blend in the melted butter and essence with the last of the flour.

3. Immediately pour into the tin and bake. After baking turn out onto a wire tray until cold. Then slice into three layers.

4. FILLING. Beat together the butter and sugar until light and fluffy. Beat in the ground almonds.

5. Beat in cream a little at a time to avoid curdling, then beat in the liqueur. Re-line the tin with greaseproof paper, then grease the paper lightly with butter.

INGREDIENTS

Metric		Imperial
	CAKE	
	3 eggs, size 3	
85g	Caster sugar	3oz
85g	Plain flour, sifted	3oz
28g	Butter, melted	1oz
	Almond essence	
	FILLING	
225g	Fresh strawberries	8oz
115g	Butter	4oz
85g	Caster sugar	3oz
85g	Ground almonds	3oz
145ml	Thick cream	5oz
90ml	Amaretto liqueur	6tbsp
	TOPPING	
145ml	Thick cream	5oz
	Toasted flaked almonds	

BAKING TIN

905g (2lb) loaf tin greased and fully lined.

BAKING

Preheated oven, 180°C or 360°F or gas mark 4
Middle shelf
25 minutes

Mary's Tips

Any other soft fruit can be used for this cake, particularly fresh raspberries, peaches, nectarines or blackberries.

It is important to allow the cake time to cool on a wire tray. Trapped steam will be retained in the cake if it is left in its tin and this will make the cake heavy. Conversely, most fruit and wedding cakes textures are improved by being kept in the tin.

6. Place the small layer of sponge into the tin and sprinkle with liqueur, then place in strawberries cut in half.

7. Cover with half the filling, then repeat step 6 and 7. Place the last slice of sponge on top, sprinkle with liqueur and chill overnight.

8. Turn out onto the serving plate. Decorate with whipped cream, strawberries and flaked almonds.

MARY FORD TITLES

101 Cake Designs

ISBN: 0 946429 00 6   320 pages
The original Mary Ford cake artistry text book. A
classic in its field, over 200,000 copies sold.

Cake Making and Decorating

ISBN: 0 946429 41 3   96 pages
Mary Ford divulges all the skills and techniques cake
decorators need to make and decorate a variety of
cakes in every medium.

Chocolate Cookbook

ISBN: 0 946429 18 9   96 pages
A complete introduction to cooking with chocolate
featuring sweets, luscious gateaux, rich desserts and
Easter Eggs.

Jams, Chutneys and Pickles

ISBN: 0 946429 33 2   96 pages
Over 70 of Mary Ford's favourite recipes for delicious
jams, jellies, pickles and chutneys with hints and tips for
perfect results.

Sugarpaste Cake Decorating

ISBN: 0 946429 10 3   96 pages
27 innovative Mary Ford cake designs illustrating royal
icing decoration on sugarpaste covered cakes.

Children's Cakes

ISBN: 0 946429 35 9   96 pages
33 exciting new Mary Ford designs and templates for
children's cakes in a wide range of mediums.

Party Cakes

ISBN: 0 946429 13 8   120 pages
36 superb party time sponge cake designs and templates
for tots to teenagers. An invaluable prop for the party
cake decorator.

Quick & Easy Cakes

ISBN: 0 946429 42 1   208 pages
The book for the busy mum. 99 new ideas for party and
special occasion cakes.

Decorative Sugar Flowers for Cakes

ISBN: 0 946429 28 6   120 pages
33 of the highest quality handcrafted sugar flowers with
cutter shapes, background information and appropriate
uses.

Sugarcraft Cake Decorating

ISBN: 0 946429 30 8   96 pages
A definitive sugarcraft book featuring an extensive
selection of exquisite sugarcraft items designed and
made by Pat Ashby.

Making Cakes for Money

ISBN: 0 946429 44 8   120 pages
The complete guide to making and costing cakes for
sale at stalls or to friends.

Home Baking with Chocolate

ISBN: 0 946429 37 5   96 pages
Over 60 tried and tested recipes for cakes, gateaux,
biscuits, confectionery and desserts. The ideal book for
busy mothers.

Desserts

ISBN: 0 946429 40 5   96 pages
Hot and cold desserts suitable for every occasion using
fresh, natural ingredients. An invaluable reference book
for the home cook, student or chef.

The Complete Book of Cake Decorating

ISBN: 0 946429 36 7   256 pages
An indispensable reference book for cake decorators,
containing totally new material covering every aspect of
cake design and artistry.

The Beginners Guide to Cake Decorating

ISBN: 0 946429 38 3   256 pages
A comprehensive guide for the complete beginner, to
every stage of the cake decorating process, including
over 150 cake designs for different occasions.